A Journey To HELL and Back

By Charlotte Russell Johnson

Foreword by Shay Youngblood,
Author of *Amazing Grace*

Black Sheep, Black Sheep

Consolation from the throne

Black Sheep, Black Sheep…
Where have you been…
Hiding with your lovers, hiding with your friends…
Black Sheep, Black Sheep…
Where have you been…
Don't you understand…
I'm your everlasting friend…

Black Sheep, Black Sheep…
Why are you in so much pain…
Black Sheep, Black Sheep…
Don't you understand…
The king's heart is in My hand…

Black Sheep, Black Sheep…
Why have you lost hope…
Black Sheep, Black Sheep…
Don't you understand…
I can help you cope…

Black Sheep, Black Sheep…
Why do you cry…
Black Sheep, Black Sheep…
Don't you understand…
I'm here to dry your eyes…

Black Sheep, Black Sheep…
Why is your head down…
Black Sheep, Black Sheep…
Don't you understand…
I'm preparing your crown…

Black Sheep, Black Sheep…
Why are you looking for temporal gain…
Black Sheep, Black Sheep…
Don't you understand…
Life in Me is eternal gain…

Black Sheep, Black Sheep...
Why worry, why fret...
Black Sheep, Black Sheep...
Don't you understand...
I know your name...
I engraved it in the palms of My hands...

Black Sheep, Black Sheep...
Why so much anguish and pain...
Black Sheep, Black Sheep...
Don't you understand...
I understand rejection...
I understand pain...

Black Sheep, Black Sheep...
Give Me your pain...
Black Sheep, Black Sheep...
Don't you understand...
You're the reason why I came...

Black Sheep, Black Sheep...
Won't you come home...
Don't you understand...
My arms are open wide...
I'm crying...
My child won't you come...

Black Sheep, Black Sheep...
Don't you understand...
I want to be your shepherd...
As only I can...

Black Sheep, Black Sheep...
There was never any lack...
Black Sheep, Black Sheep...
Don't you understand...
I was with you in HELL...
My blood brought you BACK!!!!

DEDICATION

This book is dedicated to the memory of:
Earline Alexander
October 6, 1920- January 13, 2000

She was the example of love, humility, giving, and patience, in word and deed. To her friends she was known as Byrd. But for me she was Ma'Dear. She gave us something more precious than gold, the gift of laughter. She taught us how to laugh at our mistakes, how to laugh at ourselves, and finally how to laugh in the midst of sorrow. When Ma'Dear was diagnosed with Alzheimer's, she maintained her sense of humor. Whenever she would become confused, she would turn it into a joke. When she was diagnosed with cancer, a month before her death, she showed no anger or resentment.

May we yet learn your greatest trick, how to keep smiling in the midst of the pain we feel without you.

Special thanks to La'Toya, Bobbie, Evelyn,
Margaret, and all my clients.
To all the Black Sheep.
Don't let anybody put you down.
God is able to turn it around.

La'Toya Alexandria Hall

INSIDE HELL

_____FOREWORD by Shay Youngblood

When Charlotte and I were in Junior High School sharing fried pork chop sandwiches between classes, I thought she was the luckiest girl in the world. She was smart, outspoken, well dressed, went to the most talked-about parties and could use words so sharp they could cut a new set of clothes. I wanted to be just like her. It wasn't until I read her inspirational account of her life in one sitting last fall that I discovered the pain behind her brazen attitude and the tears behind her cutting words. In *A Journey To Hell and Back,* Charlotte tells the compelling and emotionally honest story of her life. It is funny, heartbreakingly sad and filled with miracles. Her story is a testimony to the power of faith and the strength of the human spirit to survive.

Herman Russell Jr.

July 10, 1937 - July 18, 1962
My heart still bleeds for you.

PREFACE

A Journey: To Hell and Back will detail major events in my life that almost destroyed me, but instead have served to make me a stronger person and a more effective lover of God. My journey to hell led me through a fiery furnace that burned 70% of my body with 2nd and 3rd degree burns, and an over three months hospital stay where God provided personal consolation and healing. After God miraculously saved me from a life in the streets heaped with sin, my zeal for God resulted in my making additional mistakes, including renewing the abusive relationship that had almost cost my life. My desire to end this marriage resulted in my backsliding and having numerous demons move into my empty vessel, prison, exposure to drugs and AIDS. My journey from hell led me through deliverance from self-consciousness of the scars covering my body, college graduation with honors, and a ministry of restoration.

A Journey: To Hell and Back was written for those who need to know that there is life after death; there is life after failure; there is life after sickness; there is life after divorce; and there is life after prison. The purpose in writing this book is not to glorify the failure or success in my life. This book was written through my tears. The events contained within are true. Sharing them is not meant to harm or embarrass anyone. They are only shared so that those who need spiritual, emotional, and physical healing may be encouraged to seek life after hell.

Over twelve years ago God told me to tell the whole story, because this was an opportunity to glorify Him. My limited understanding didn't comprehend the magnitude of what He meant. Over the years, He has made His instructions increasingly clearer. I offer my life as a source of encouragement to every mother who has a wayward child, every woman who has been abused, every teenager who is confused, every person who has given up hope, every person trapped in a comfort zone, and every person who has lost faith. Rather than curse the darkness, I have chosen to light candles, and thus begin to rise from the ashes of a life that literally burned itself out.

The Bible tells us clearly that we overcome by the words of our testimony and the blood of the Lamb. God has placed within my heart the desire to share these events so that others may be helped. Yet, He alone has been able to give me the strength to share the things that I would rather forget. It is my desire that in sharing my struggle, and exposing the source of my pain, others will be encouraged to hold on when all looks hopeless. My life can only be described as a trip to the pits of hell and a remarkable testimony of the Love of God that bought me back. This is not an attempt to glorify the devil or his angels, but to expose him for the thief and robber that he is. Jesus truly has power over death, hell, and the grave.

My prayer is that your life will be enriched by something written in this book. If all I have found from the tragedies of my life is bitterness, resentment and tears, my pain has been wasted, but if I can share my pain and the victory that has come from it, then the pain can't hold me hostage. It was a hard task to expose the source and root of my pain, but if others are encouraged to hold in spite of odds that seem insurmountable, what I endured and overcame has everlasting value. This book is a testimony of the wonderful saving grace of my Lord and Savior, Jesus Christ, who loves us enough to even reach into the pits of hell and with the redemptive power of His blood snatch us back from hell's grip. Not only does He have the power to snatch us from the pits of hell, but He alone has the power to work all things out for the good of those who love the Lord and who are the called according to His purpose. I could never repay Him for all that He has done for me, but at least in my obedience in writing this book, I have acknowledged the debt.

The names of some individuals in this book have been changed to respect their rights to privacy. Other names have been changed to protect those who love them.

All scripture references are from the King James Bible, unless otherwise noted.

_____Introduction by Earline Hall

A Journey: To Hell and Back is a gripping saga of a young woman's journey from adolescence to adulthood at an accelerated pace. This book is an exploration of a troubled teen's journey into the underworld to emerge as an independent, confident, and self-assured woman. Pitfalls, tragedy, and trials that lure a young honor student into the mean streets of Atlanta and finally, New York mark the story.

The story is a modern day version of Dante's Inferno. Each layer of Hell corresponds with a new low in the protagonist's life. Finally from within the very bowels of Hell, she cries out to the Lord for salvation. This spiritual epiphany becomes a turning point in her life, thrusting her forward from Hell.

This book will appeal to a very diverse audience. It's easy flow and intricate plot twists, will serve to hold the attention of readers who prefer books from non-spiritual genres. The tremendous suffering and miraculous ending of this book will offer hope and comfort for anyone suffering from loneliness, heartache, or disappointment. It provides a realistic and human perspective on many social topics such as teenage rebellion and pregnancy, domestic violence, divorce, AIDS, substance abuse, prostitution, and the legal system. This book is a necessity for anyone who has been a part of or will work with any of these populations. They say you don't know a person until you've walked a mile in their shoes. Author Charlotte Johnson generously invites you to borrow hers.

Charlotte Russell
Smiling… masquerading….

THE PATH TO HELL

The Devil has come to steal, kill, and destroy.

It has often been said that the road to hell is paved with good intentions. This is cliché not a fact. This road was paved with pain, deceit, insecurity, pride, stubbornness, foolishness, and disobedience, more appropriately known as sin. This road seems to have no beginning or perhaps its beginning was before my birth. A series of events before my birth would serve to breed a root of bitterness in me that would send my life spinning out of control. It wasn't the circumstances of my birth that had such a profound effect on most of my life. The manner in which I learned of these circumstances is what cut me into crumbling pieces.

One of my earliest memories is that of being at the Well Baby Clinic in Warren Williams Apartments. Warren Williams is a public housing project in Columbus, Georgia. During one of our visits to the clinic, I remember the nurse calling me Charlotte Alexander. There were two Alexander babies at the clinic with my aunt that day. One was my uncle Carlton Alexander, and the other baby was me. There is less than three weeks difference in our ages. The nurse was confused as to which Alexander baby was being seen. We were both receiving examinations. There was no explanation for this memory, because I must have been very young. I remember that my aunt Pickle (Carolyn) explained that my name was Charlotte Russell. Somehow, even at this early age, I understood that at some point in my life, my name was Alexander. I pondered this in my heart for years. During my seventh grade year this mystery would be thoroughly, publicly, and maliciously explained to me.

Being a teenager is an extremely emotional and difficult period in anyone's life. Additional complications would make this time in my life even more complicated. This was the first year for integration in the Muscogee County School System. It was a time of violence, resistance, racial uprisings, and confusion. This was added to the natural confusion already present in my life. The teenage years are a time when you don't know exactly where or how you fit into your environment. You're no longer a child but you're not an adult either. These are very fragile and delicate years. They may be termed as the years that only the strong survive. Youth requires an extreme amount of nurture, love, and patience during these years. This is often difficult to balance with appropriate discipline. These years are during a season that we seek independence, while seeking a place of belonging. This wasn't going to happen for me, for many years. Circumstances beyond my control would make me the target of jealousy in its cruelest form.

When I was born we lived in Warren Williams Apartments, and this is where most of the early years of my life were spent. The projects in Columbus were remodeled regularly and well maintained, and by no stretch of imagination could they be classified as a dump for low-income people. Most of the people in Warren Williams had lived there for years or closer to forever. Everybody knew each other, and everybody knew everybody's business. It was here that the foundation was laid for my journey to hell. Rather than our living there being a financial necessity, it was my mother's choice. This housing project represented safety and security to her, because she had spent most of her life there. We had moved out of Warren Williams for three years, during my third through six grade years. However, my grandmother still resided in Warren Williams and we spent a considerable amount of time with her during this period. Ma'Dear kept us most of the time when my mother was working.

During the three years that we were away from Warren Williams, we had moved to a better neighborhood, or it was supposed to be a better neighborhood. There were several attempted burglaries at this address, and our bicycles were stolen regularly. The last attempted burglary was successful. My mother was awakened by the sound of broken glass. She ran into the kitchen to discover an arm coming through the kitchen window. She was able to escape through the living room door, in an attempt to get help from a neighbor. The burglar chased her down the street. He caught her, shortly before she made it to her destination, knocking her down on a grassy hill. While she struggled to get away, he cut her across her arm with a knife. Barking dogs disturbed the quietness of the night, serving to rescue her from the attacker. The continuos barking alerted her friends. They came to the door to investigate the commotion. The confusion was enough to cause the burglar to release her. When the burglar ran back up the street towards our home, Mama was able to make it to her friend's house. There she called the police and my uncle, Teddy.

During the interval, the burglar returned to our home. My younger sister, Crystal and I were still asleep, in separate bedrooms. After entering my bedroom, he approached my bed, careful not to awaken me before he had me secured within his grip. Sleepy and dazed, the eyes of this stranger looming directly over my face, staring directly into my eyes startled and confused me. Placing his hand firmly over my mouth, he forced me to scream silent screams that were never heard. Grabbing me around the neck with his forearm, he began dragging me from the bedroom and towards the backdoor of the house. I managed to remain wrapped in a sheet. As he was dragging me out the back door, a blast of light shone in his face. It was the headlights of a taxicab that was pulling into the driveway. My uncle had just arrived in the taxicab. The police hadn't yet arrived. The burglar or would be rapist let go of me, and began to run, with my uncle in hot pursuit. The police arrived some time later and joined the search. Darkness aided the burglar's escape. After chasing him through a nearby neighborhood, they were unable to catch him. He had gotten away with a small amount of change from the top of the dresser, my lunch money, approximately fifty cents. My sister slept through the whole incident. This incident would leave my mother resolved to return to the safety of the project. We were moving back to the project, but not because we were struggling financially. In fact, financial we were thriving. This is one of the things that would serve to make me a misfit.

There is another early memory that has lingered with me, Gussie Pope Chubby Decker Shop. Chubby Decker may be imagined, but not the shop. This was a dimly lit shop with no attractively displayed mannequins, bright colors, or stylish trends. There was nothing appealing about the shop or the name of the shop. The most distinguishing feature about the shop was that the clothes were as wide as they were long. This was a shop that sold clothes for fat children, like me. This was the store that catered to my needs through my sixth grade year, because I was extremely over weight. While I appreciate the need for the shop, if there is a need for any store to be attractive, it's one that caters to this clientele.

A startling event would occur the summer before I entered Junior High School, Miss Fat would become Miss Fine. Almost miraculously, the pounds began to drop off, without a special diet or any effort on my part. By the time I began my seventh grade year, I was wearing a size nine. No more Gussie Pope! I could shop at the finest stores in Columbus, Georgia, again. My mother was really excited about my going to Junior High School. For more than one reason, I needed a new wardrobe. Mama thought going to Junior High merited a new wardrobe, including clothes and expensive shoes. Every weekend, the shopping sprees were on. The dresses took on a new look; they may still have been wider than they were long. However, they were also short and shorter. Ma'Dear hemmed them for me to show just the right amount of my legs. The shortness of my dresses sparked a wave of jealousy and conversations that began on the first day of junior high school.

This was also the time when I developed a love for Cocoa Butter, in my efforts to ensure there were no marks on my body. The things that were a part of my daily ritual were Cocoa Butter Lotion, Cocoa Butter Bath Oil Beads, Cocoa Butter Soap, and pure Cocoa Butter. This may give the appearance that I was being conceited, but actually, I was still carrying all the words said about me when I was overweight. The words didn't stop with the weight loss, the message just changed. I was still convinced that I was unattractive. The Cocoa Butter was my effort to improve my appearance. My attention was focused on making sure that my legs looked good. I was still very dissatisfied with my appearance. I had learned that there was one way to get the attention that I was desperately searching for. My short dresses kept males of all ages looking, and making passes at me. Lust had nothing to do with attractiveness. It didn't matter that they had only one interest. I thought that it was kind of amusing. I had learned to accept this as one of the realities of life, since a person that my mother trusted to come into our family had molested me years earlier. This man not only violated her trust; he violated her child. Knowing that Mama loved this man, the secret was kept for many years.

The seventh grade was marked by change, and not just in my appearance. This was the first time in three years that I would attend school with people from Warren Williams. It was the first time that classes would be separated based on academic scoring. I was placed in academically advanced classes. As the only Black in some of these classes, again I wouldn't fit in with the people from my neighborhood. It would have been easier if the Whites hadn't accepted me, but it was Blacks. There wasn't a problem with the people in the classes. This helped to make me a further outcast with the people that I would walk home with each day. There would be days that I would be forced to fight and had no idea what brought the fight on. There would be many cruel and heartless things said about me and to me on these journeys home. I learned to pretend that the words didn't matter. Words don't hurt; they destroy. They murder from inside your heart.

Oh! Back to my early memory of the Well Baby Clinic, the memory that didn't make any sense. The trips home were often emotionally painful for me. On one of these trips home, someone explained to me that my mother and father weren't married when I was born. In front of everybody walking to Warren Williams, one of the girls called me Charlotte Alexander. When I didn't respond, someone else asked her why she had called me by this name. Everybody in the group had already heard the story, that is with the exception of me. She was more than glad to oblige with an explanation. She explained that my parents weren't married when I was born. My name had indeed been Charlotte Alexander for a short period of time. Again, as I was accustomed to doing, I pretended that it didn't matter. This would serve as the catalyst that not only broke my heart, shattering the one thing in my life that was perfect, my memory of my father, but would also cause my mother's heart to be pierced through with great sorrow for many years.

I am weary with my groaning: all night I make my bed to swim; I water my coach with tears. Mine eyes are consumed because of grief; it waxeth old because of mine enemies. Psalm 6:6-7

I had always imagined my father as perfect and faultless. You know one of those like Fred McMurray on "My Three Sons." I had only two memories of ever seeing him. The first one was of him coming up the stairs at Ma'Dear's house, while my baby-sitter was giving me a bath in the bathroom at the top of the stairs. On another occasion, I was outside near the end of the apartment building when he came home on leave to visit us. We were still living with Ma'Dear then. Both times we were elated to see each other.

In my deepest times of loneliness, I imagined what my life would be like if I had been given the opportunity to know my father. My images of him were the only perfect thing in my life. I felt cheated, deprived, and robbed of all semblance of normalcy by the person who had murdered him when I was three years old. I often wondered if this murderer knew what he had done to my life, if he had any understanding of the depth of the pain that he had forced into my life. I couldn't understand how my mother could forgive the person who had single-handedly wrecked my life. Shortly after murdering my father, the murderer wrote my mother a letter apologizing for murdering my father. Mama quickly decided to accept his plea for forgiveness. I never received a courtesy letter, requesting my forgiveness. No one gave more than a fleeting thought to how this death would affect a three-year-old child. This was churning in my mind while I waited for Mama to return home from work.

My picture perfect imaginary life was about to be shattered. When my mother returned home from work, I wanted answers. In the midst of my anger and pain, she was confronted with what I had been told. I was sure they were mistaken about the circumstances and what I had been told was a mistake. At this time, I only knew a few details of my father's death. The conversation that would ensue would cause me to resent my mother at a time when I would desperately need her support. I would be left alone and isolated with my pain, while pretending each day this information had no effect on me. I would begin to grieve for a person who had been deceased for more than ten years. It was as if my father died for a second time. How do you tell someone that you have just begun the grieving process for someone who died before you even understood the meaning of life or death? What is a teenager's understanding of grief? Who do you tell about the pain causing a war in your mind? Who will understand that you aren't losing your mind? I began a facade of pretending everything was fine, yet inside I was dying. I was taking another step towards hell.

My mother's answers weren't what I expected, needed or wanted. She explained the circumstances that led to her pregnancy. I wasn't really concerned about the circumstances. That was nothing new; most of the people living in the project were from single parent homes. What was going over and over in my mind was the conversation on the way home. The whole gang was laughing when I was told. Why was I allowed to find out this way? I had learned this information in a way that was a deliberate attempt to hurt and embarrass me. This attempt had succeeded on both fronts. My mother would attempt to explain her situation. However, her answers were a threat to my image of my perfect father. I would begin a mission to prove she was at fault and to preserve the only semblance of perfection in my life.

My mother had kept every letter that my father had ever written her. She had duffel bags full of these letters, in her bedroom closet. My father was Airborne and had been stationed in Fort Campbell, Kentucky at the time of his murder. He had written my mother regularly during the times that they were separated. I decided that I would read each and every letter that he had sent her, and make my own evaluation. The times that she was working provided the perfect opportunity for me to carry out my mission. I was determined to find my answers, at any cost. For hours each day, I read these letters until I was sure I had read each of them thoroughly. The longer I read the letters, the more I blamed my mother for their separation. I would often sit alone in my misery, in the dark, playing sad songs, and thinking about my father. The mirror over my dresser in my bedroom served as the place where I often saw my father's face looking down on me when I was hurting the most. The thoughts were always the same.

"My life would be so different if he had lived."

We had no real relationship with either of my father's parents. This left me without a tangible foundation to build a bridge to knowing my father. If his family had been an active part of my life, perhaps I would have known my father through their memories. This was another part of my confusion. Why wouldn't they want to know the children of their dead son and deceased brother? This confusion would get worse the next year.

In some of my loneliest moments of reflections, I wrote poems about my feelings. The things that I couldn't express audibly, the pains that .I couldn't share with anyone were written down. Mama was an immaculate housekeeper. Our home had fine, expensive, and elaborate furniture. Even the curtains in the kitchen and bathroom were made by the best interior decorator in Columbus, the same one that decorated the most luxurious homes in Columbus.

Posting my poems all around the room, distracting from the decor of the room was unacceptable. The room was furnished with an exquisite Early American bedroom suit that Mama had just purchased for my birthday. This made me mad, too. I had requested a waterbed, which was much cheaper. However, I found two places that wouldn't bother Mama. One place was over the window air conditioner in my room. The window was covered by custom-made drapes and could be easily closed when we had visitors. The second home for my poems was in a corner of the room, near the head of my bed, behind a glass table that was also a lamp. Part of the metal ornamentation of the lamp was flowers in various colors that extended from the base of the table. This gave me an idea of making a flower garden around the base of the wall. My flowers were made out of construction paper in a variety of colors. The flowers contained the words to my poems. This represented what I wished my life was like. One of the poems that still stands out in my memory was simply entitled *Dreams, Hopes and Wishes*. These were things that I understood well.

Dreams, Hopes, Wishes
I often sit and stare at the world,
And dream dreams,
And hope hopes,
And wish wishes,
And lately,
I listen to a mellow song,
As it dances a beautiful dance for me,
But these moments,
These moments never,
Never seem to last too long,
For after the dreams, hopes, and wishes,

And after the singing dancing melody,
And after you and me and a stolen moment of happiness,
After a glimpse at the timeless Natural Universe,
Comes the stark reality of today,
His ugly face pressed firmly against mine,
Washing away wishes of yesterday's dreams,
Crumbling hopes,
Destroying wishes,
Yes it's too late to turn back now,
For it was only just,
A dream!

As my struggle to fit in continued, I made more foolish mistakes. We began petty stealing from "Old Mr. Jessie Binns' Grocery." He was a city councilman who had a small grocery store across from Warren Williams for numerous years. We stopped by his store in each morning on our way to school, and again each afternoon on the way home each day. We would buy a little something and steal a little something. He knew that we were stealing, but he couldn't watch all of us at the same time. I would usually steal cigarettes. I didn't smoke, so this became my hustle. I would sale cigarettes for a nickel each. This would provide me with additional money for my Saturday shopping trips. Shopping had become the way that I dealt with my pain. My mother gave me an allowance each week, but I was saving this money, too. The third way I was getting money was by keeping my lunch money. Mama wouldn't fill out the free lunch forms, so I filled them out each year, forged forms because I didn't qualify for free lunches.

The money that I had each week wasn't enough for me to buy the type of clothes that I wanted, but it was enough to put them on layaway. However, I had no intention of getting the clothes out of layaway. The people at Kiddie Shoppe knew my mother. She was a regular customer, and always had several layaways. I just added a few more layaways in her name. When I didn't have enough money to make the deposit on the layaway, I would request that they call the manager for approval. He would approve the layaways, since my mother always got them out. I knew at least a couple of times a month she was going to pick up layaways. It wasn't that she was unaware that I was going to Kiddie Shoppe each weekend; she just accepted it because she liked the clothes that I was picking out.

Mama worked in the downtown area, and I was actually supposed to be coming to visit her at work. It was easy for me to ride the bus a block pass my bus stop and then walk back to visit her, after I finished shopping.

She kept warning me to stop going in the store, but I wouldn't stop. I knew that if she saw the clothes that she would like them, and if she liked them she was going to buy them. I took this for granted. At this time, there were rich kids attending school with us, but this shopping habit of mine led to a girl from the project being voted the best-dressed girl in school.

Once we, too, were foolish and disobedient. We were misled by others and became slaves to many wicked desire and evil pleasures. Our lives were full of evil and envy. We hated others, and they hated us. Titus 3:3-4 NLT

My best friend since sixth grade was Peggy. As a team, we were awesome, or should I say trouble. Everything bad that I didn't do Peggy did. Between the two of us, we were doing basically everything. Mama was working, and I was supposed to be taking care of the house. I was also supposed to be keeping my younger sister Crystal. Mama had no idea who she was leaving her house with. There was always plenty of food at our house, enough to share.

Sometimes, when we went to the Commissary, we got three buggies, one for Mama, one for me, and one for Crystal. Mama would tell us that we could write a list of ten major things that we wanted. This was funny. Even though we prepared the lists with only ten special things to purchase, it never worked out that way when we got to the Commissary. As Mama would be pushing on ahead of us, we were hiding things in the buggies. We were sure that she wouldn't put anything back. When it came to the chips' section, we got one of every kind of chips that they had, to include different brands. The chips were Mama's idea. When she began to check out, we turned our heads away from her. When we got home Mama would be embarrassed, and tried to wait until there were no neighbors outdoors, before we took the grocery in the house. This led to our house being the hang out house when Mama was at work.

During my seventh grade year, I had become interested in older men, or should I say guys in high school. A relationship with a high school senior would develop during this time. This relationship would only serve to further destroy my faltering self-esteem down further. It would be an on off relationship for a number of years. It was on whenever he wanted it on. Whenever Mama was at work, Crystal and I were suppose to stay in the house, without company. This was easy enough to fix. Mama knew that teenagers loved to talk on the telephone, and Call-Waiting hadn't been invented yet. This made it easy to just take the telephone off the hook when I slipped off to the YMCA. Crystal played on the playground while I was inside with my friends. This was almost every day. Whenever I was at home, I had company. There was an old lady that lived on an apartment row that faced our apartment. She was supposed to keep an eye on us while Mama was at work. She was so nosy that I think that she volunteered for the job.

One day when I had three boys (all high school seniors) in the house, I heard the key turning in the back door. This was Mama slipping back home, trying to catch me. Miss Nosy had called her at work to tell her that I had company in the house. Before she got in the house, they had run out the front door and hid in the ditch across the street. Mama knew her house and could tell that someone had walked through the living room, but they got away. However, they had just gotten to the house and nothing was going on. I was involved with one of them, Skin. However, on this day, they were really looking for something to eat.

The YMCA was our favorite hangout, for awhile. This was where I met Skin. There were often dances at the "Y," but Mama wouldn't allow me to go without an escort. This wasn't going to hinder me. There were two things that I always had, money and a plan. My plan was that my uncle would pick me up, telling my mother he would take me to the dances and bring me back. Actually, he escorted me across the street to Jessie Binns' Grocery, and after making sure that the coast was clear, he went one direction and I went another. At a prearranged time, he met me back in the same spot, and escorted me back to the door. This was a paid escort service.

During the eighth grade year, my antics increased and at school there was also a lot of mischief going on. Peggy decided to come to school one-day drunk, and I had the task of convincing the staff that she was just feeling bad. There was only one problem with this, Peggy didn't want to cooperate, and kept trying to help them figure out the real source of the problem. We made it through the day without them discovering what was wrong. In the classroom, we were also terrors. There was one classroom that we were in together. Sharon Youngblood was also in this class. Having Peggy and me in the same classroom was a mistake.

My Aunt Pickle (Carolyn) had taught me a game and I taught it to everyone else in the class. The game began, "Pussy Willow was walking down the street one day and stumbled upon a pile of bull..." Another person would respond, "Who...?" The person in the room would answer the question using a different animal. The next person would interrupt, "Bull...," using the word that described the original pile. The "S" word went behind the name of each animal that was then credited with owning the pile.

The pattern repeated itself. Each time, a mumbled response came from the opposite side of the room. The teacher was mortified, because we were muttering these horrible things under our breath. She was unable to figure out where the words were coming from, since the voices were going from one side of the room to the other. She never sent anybody to the office; I guess she understood that we really didn't mean any harm.

There was also something else we did in this classroom. We brought food each day and passed snacks around the room. We were having a private party while the teacher was trying to teach. One of my favorite items was a ham sandwich with mayonnaise, lettuce, tomatoes, and sliced pickles. Sharon brought fried pork chop sandwiches with mustard. This teacher had no idea how to regain ownership of the classroom.

To make matters worse for this teacher, it snowed that year. It rarely snowed in Columbus. This time the snow began while we were at school, and in her classroom. We began throwing snowballs in the hall at everybody, including the teachers. Everybody was sliding across the hall struggling to maintain his or her balance on the wet and slippery floor. I had a bright idea. Deciding to play a trick on the teacher, I slipped a snowball into the classroom while the teacher was struggling to assist in regaining order in the hall. Immediately, I needed a place to hide the snowball. Her bag looked like a good place to put it. When she returned to the room, she reached in her bag for the roll book.

Frantic she screamed, "Who ever did this has ruined my grade book. If I can't read your grades, everybody will get an F."

It didn't seem like such a bright idea, but nobody said a word. They liked the things that I was teaching them. Somehow, the teacher survived the year.

In the midst of all of the confusion in my life, I had managed to maintain my grades. This was something that I prided myself on. This was about to change too. I was assigned my first term paper. Countless hours would go into researching and preparing this paper. This masterpiece was finally completed and submitted to the instructor. I have long since forgotten her name, but I will forever remember her face and the location of the classroom. To my utter dismay, my perfect paper was returned with my first "D." The comment read, "This paper sounds bookish. It's too good. I don't believe that you wrote it." This caused me to become angry and slightly depressed. My normally docile mother who had watched me laboring over the paper tried to intervene with the teacher to no avail. The teacher was adamant; she wouldn't give me the grade that I deserved. I decided that I would never work for a grade this hard again. Another step towards hell was taken.

> *No discipline is enjoyable while it is happening - it is painful! But afterward there will be a quite harvest of right living for those who are trained in the way.* Hebrews 12:11-12 NLT

During this time my efforts to fit in would escalate. There were a number of girls at school who boasted of going to nearby nightclubs on the weekends without anyone questioning their age. They said this was a lot of fun. These were people that I didn't even hang out with. I would take on this challenge to get into one of these clubs. It didn't matter that I didn't drink alcoholic beverages or even particularly like to dance. There was no one at these clubs that I even wanted to date. Nevertheless, I began going to these clubs on the weekends. I didn't even enjoy going. Most of the time, I wouldn't even sit down. Strangely, while there, I never saw any of the girls from school who were supposed to be frequenting these clubs. This didn't stop me from going back.

My mother eventually discovered these trips to the nightclub. Some nosy person dipping into my business told her about my trips. One of my uncles who was four years older than I was (he was sixteen) would chase me back home. It didn't matter that he wasn't old enough to be at these clubs either. By this time, I had really begun to resent any form of discipline. After one of my trips to the nightclubs, my uncle would beat me in the backyard with a belt. This was the same uncle that had been my paid escort. This only increased my resentment, and almost cost me my life.

My life was so miserable; I decided that I just wanted to die. Actually, I had been in a mild depression for awhile. No one recognized the depression. I found a bottle of diet pills and proceeded to take them all, choosing to leave one pill remaining. For some sick reason, I decided that I would leave my mother one pill for the next day. This would allow her enough time to get her prescription refilled. Why I thought the day she found her child dead she would be worried about a diet pill, I don't know. In a very short time, I became confused and disoriented.

> *For we would not brethren, have you ignorant of our trouble which came upon us in Asia, that we were pressed out of measure, above strength, insomuch that we despaired even of life: But we had the sentence of death in ourselves, that we should not trust ourselves, but in God which raised the dead: who delivered us from so great death, and doth deliver: in whom we trust that he will yet deliver.*
> II Corinthians 1:8-10

This was my first attempt at suicide. Sometime later, I was rushed to Martin Army Hospital and my stomach was pumped. They did the usual, bringing a psychiatrist in to talk to me. I don't remember the conversations, but I know I didn't tell them what was wrong with me. Actually, I didn't know what was wrong. I was just unhappy with my life. After several days, I was released from the hospital. There was no follow-up counseling or treatment. A couple of months later, I tried to take my life again with a different type of pills. This only resulted in my spending an extended period with my head over the toilet. From this point on, it would be difficult for me to swallow pills for any reason without becoming sick on the stomach. There would be a lot of speculation in the neighborhood about my hospital stay. They were all wrong. The strongest rumor was that I had an abortion. I was getting closer to hell.

There was a desperate need for someone to love me, just as I was, without expecting me to change. Lust was the closest that I was coming to love. I was tired of being asked what I was going to do with my life. I didn't want to be encouraged to go college. It wasn't the encouragement that bothered me. The method bothered me. These Sunday messages that were meant to encourage me were actually put downs of other people. People who lacked a college education were described as nothing. The necessity of living in house was also stressed. This was meant to be a put down of my mother. To me snobs were worse than the people they attempted to look down on were. In my mind no one accepted me for who I was. Unconsciously, I think, I decided to give them a real "Black Sheep" in their family.

During my ninth grade year, things would move to a new level. Skin (my on and off whatever) had enlisted in the army, and was getting ready to leave for basic training in a few weeks. I hadn't seen him or been involved with him in months. This was by my choice. I had tired of his games. He still hung out at the YMCA. For a while, the "Y" had been the hot spot, but presently it was dying out. As I was walking past the "Y" one night, I saw Skin leaving. He offered to give me a ride home. Although, I knew that he didn't mean me any good, I still had a soft spot in my heart for him, so I accepted the ride. Warren Williams was only a few blocks from the "Y". However, this trip would detour across town to his apartment, and leave me with something to remember him by forever. The Rhythm Method had been my favorite method of birth control. He would choose to ignore my warnings that this was the wrong time of the month.

In my sick mind and afraid of his response, I would come up with an even sicker way to handle this situation. I didn't want to give him the opportunity to deny my child. Since we were corresponding regularly after he left for basic training, I would immediately tell him about the pregnancy. However, afraid of another heartache, it would be several months before I would tell him that he was the father of my baby. At fourteen, in the ninth grade, I had made the decision that I would take care of my own baby. I quickly relayed this to Skin. I wouldn't need anything from him. This one was on me. Finally, I would have "someone to love me just for me." I wanted everybody to know, and when the principal called me to the office to question me about the rumors, I proudly announced that I was indeed pregnant. As a result of this announcement, two months into my pregnancy, I was expelled from high school. There were other girls in the school who were pregnant, but my fault was in acknowledging the pregnancy. The rumors were flying through the neighborhood again. Mama came home from work each day and took to her bed. She cried for days that seemed endless.

During the summer, I went to work for a summer youth program. This wasn't enough money to take care of a baby, but the job would enable me to buy some of the basics before my baby was born. My mouth would cause me to loose this job. I had become a real champion of the "underdog." This summer, I was working at the recreation center in Warren Williams. Part of my duties consisted of passing out free lunches to children in the neighborhood. Each day the recreation director would save back a case of lunches for people that she favored adults who didn't meet the eligibility requirements. When the children continued to arrive, she would tell them all the lunches were gone. This irritated me for several weeks. One day when she said this, I reminded her of the case that was still in the kitchen. That evening she told me that I had gotten too big (advanced in my pregnancy) to continue working.

My uncle Carlton and I had always been inseparable. When one was hurt, the other cried. If you did something to one the other responded. In the first grade, we had been in the same classroom. Carlton stuttered profusely during the first couple of years that we were in school. He was very self-conscience of his speaking pattern. Our first grade teacher made the mistake of forcing him to speak. One day she asked Carlton what was his mother's name.

Stuttering, he said, "Ma'Dear."

She asked him again, while I sat listening, "What's her real name?"

This time he responded, "Byrd."

She asked him again, "What your mother's real name?"

This time he responded in tears, "Ma'Dear."

I was getting really angry, knowing that he didn't want to keep talking in front of the class.

After she noticed him crying, she made the mistake of asking me, "Charlotte, what is your grandmother's name?"

Angrily I responded, "Didn't he just tell you, Ma'Dear?"

I knew who to tell if she said anything else, Pickle. She didn't make the mistake of asking me twice. She sent for my Uncle Teddy who was in a higher grade, and sent a note home by him, explaining how I had talked to her. My Mama never found out about this incident.

Whenever anybody said anything to us, whether it was an adult or child, the only person we told was Pickle. Without asking for another side of the story, Pickle would come to our rescue. Pickle had the school crossing guard, and my kindergarten teacher at Claflin Elementary bringing me candy for three years, until I transferred to another school. This was because they were rude to me on separate occasions. When I told Pickle, she went to the school and told them that she would beat the mess out of them if they said anything else to me. Pickle didn't say it quite this nicely. We didn't tell my mother about any of the trouble that we got into. We kept everything from Mama, because she would punish me if she knew what we were doing. Mama never got angry with anybody.

One night when I was at one of my friend's house, Carlton knocked on the door and asked me to come outdoors. This was around this same time that Carlton and his friends began experimenting with Acid. A group of his friends were waiting outside. We walked a short distance away and he explained that one of the boys, Dwayne, had said that my baby was going to be born ugly. Carlton handed me a dog chain. While he held a knife on Dwayne, I beat him with the chain. Finally, he was able to escape, running home. When he got home he reported this to his mother. His mother sent his father to my grandmother's house to tell my grandmother what we had done. Of course, we made sure that he talked to Pickle. He never mentioned the purpose for his visit. He was too busy flirting with Pickle. It wouldn't have done any good for him to tell Pickle, and probably would have made her grab a knife at him. Pickle had taught us early on to keep bricks near the house for protection.

Pickle instructed us, "If anybody bothers you, hit them with a brick, and run to me. I'll beat the 'H' out of them."

On October 2, 1974, at age 15, my **first** pregnancy resulted in the birth of an 8lb 5oz baby girl, Earline. She was and still is the most beautiful baby that I had ever seen. My baby was born less than an hour after I arrived at the hospital. That morning while I was eating a breakfast that consisted of smoked sausage, scrambled eggs with cheese, cheese grits, hot chocolate, and a pomegranate for dessert, I began to have indigestion. During my pregnancy, I was careful not to take any medications that weren't approved by a doctor. Ma'Dear told me to eat a spoon of mustard for the indigestion, but this didn't work. It was always difficult to reach the medical staff at Martin Army Hospital. This day was no different. After I was unable to reach the hospital by telephone, Ma'Dear called Mama to tell her what was happening. Mama decided that it was best to take me to the hospital.

When we arrived on the labor and delivery ward, the nurse informed me that my baby would be born within the hour. This scared Mama and me. I was shaking so bad that I couldn't push during the labor. This was a day that I had feared since I found out Martin Army believed in natural childbirth. I had been pressured early in my pregnancy to abort my baby, and had flatly refused. When I went for my first examination at Martin Army, they told me that I would have natural childbirth unless it became necessary for me to have a cesarean birth. This made me consider the abortion momentarily, until they told me that they wouldn't put me to sleep to have the abortion either. Scared already by the unknown and all the horror stories that I had heard about childbirth, the women screaming in the ward made me change my mind about having a baby. It was too late to change the course. I was scared that soon I would be hurting like these women. My legs and hands were trembling so much that I couldn't help with the delivery process. Mama was constantly beating my hands trying to reassure me.

"It's going to be all right baby."

My baby was born within the hour, and the pains never got any worse than the pains of indigestion. Skin only came back a couple of times over the years, and the times that he was in town were the only times that he did anything for my baby. My daughter, now an adult, would like her father referred to by his Christian name James Gosha.

A few weeks after my baby's birth, I would begin attending Columbus High School, starting the ninth grade over. This would be a new beginning in several ways. My Saturday shopping trips were now limited. My mother had another person to provide for. I resented my weekly shopping trips coming to an end. I would still be able to go shopping, but not as frequently. On one of my shopping trips, I would meet a guy working at Newberry's Department Store. There was something about him that I liked. This wasn't so much physical attraction. There was just something about him that impressed me, and lingered on my mind. I later saw him at school, and my interest was further peaked. My investigation found that he was extremely smart, or should I say a nerd by most definitions. This guy who didn't fit in either was appealing to me. This was the first time that I was seriously attracted to someone near my own age range. It didn't take much for me to build a stormy relationship with "Mr. Wright."

Barry touched me in a way no one before or after him ever did. This wasn't based on physical attraction or lust. He stimulated my mind and my spirit, challenging me intellectually in a way no one ever had. With him, there was no jealousy or threats because I had a semi-intelligent thought. My relationship with Barry brought out the best in me, and a lot of my insecurities. He didn't quite bring out the worst in me, but hints of what was hidden within would seep out.

The teachers loved Mr. Wright. He was on the debate team. This team had a lot of extra privileges. Periodically, they were allowed to travel out of town for debates. There were three guys on the team that were outstanding, and they were all friends. An opportunity presented itself for the three friends to travel to Atlanta for a competition that would last several days. The debate team coach was a female teacher. This would require the school to pay for at least two rooms. A plan was in the making. Barry and Wayne had girlfriends. Bran didn't have a girlfriend. When Barry and Wayne presented the teacher with the plan, she was willing to accommodate their request. They planned to bring their girlfriends along for the trip. The parents of the girls would be told that the school was allowing the girls to participate in the trip. Actually, I doubt that the school had any idea that additional people would be making this trip. They definitely had no idea of the sleeping arrangements that we were making. The teacher assured our parents that we would be safe in her care, and that she would carefully monitor our behavior.

After leaving the school for the trip to Atlanta, the teacher stopped at a nearby liquor store to buy booze for the trip. This was for her and Bran, the third member of the debate team. The teenage couples had no interest in drinking alcohol. We had other plans. When we arrived in Atlanta, we checked into a beautiful hotel. Indeed there were two adjoining rooms, a single suite and a double suite. This was better than we had planned. The couples were going in the double suite, and Bran would have to stay in the room with the teacher.

Barry was very caring, loving, and responsible for a sixteen-year-old. We shared everything. There was no separateness or selfishness. There were cards, flowers, jewelry, and gifts for all occasions. Sometimes there were gifts just because he was Mr. Wright. He loved my daughter, and began assisting me with this responsibility. There were days when we left school, if Barry only had a couple of dollars, we stopped by the drug store to get a can of formula for Earline. For Earline's first Easter, Barry bought her the biggest Easter basket in Newberry's. The basket was at least 4' feet tall. We removed everything from the inside of it and sat Earline in the basket. I wished with all my heart that I had waited and that he had been her father.

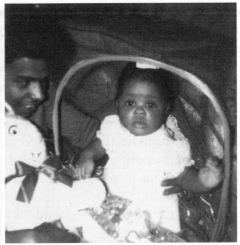

I was still carrying a lot of excess baggage. He immediately began buying me clothes and jewelry. He was also buying for my baby. After having waited so long to find someone to accept me just for myself, I was desperately afraid of losing him. My emotions would elevate from one extreme to another, from clutching to pushing him away, then desperate attempts to reconcile the relationship. Whenever he made me angry, I would give him back everything that he had bought me. He would give me everything back when we reconciled. Finally, one day after we had been arguing again, I had my mother to drive me to his house. I threw everything that he had given me in his front yard. Fed up with this, he threw away everything that I had dumped in the yard. He made his point. When I found out that I wouldn't be getting these things back, I cried, but I never tried this again with anyone.

During this time Barry and I were skipping school at least on a weekly basis. We would stay at school for almost half of the day, making sure all of our class work was current. He would write me a note requesting that I be excused from school early. My mother supposedly signed this note. I would write one for him supposedly signed by his grandmother. Knowing that we couldn't report to the office together, we allowed fifteen minutes intervals between our individual trips to the office. After this we met up in the park. Occasionally, when there was nothing important pending at school, we spent the whole day at his grandmother's house. Of course this was without her knowledge, while she was at work.

We had been making plans to attend the prom for several months. One day, Barry announced that he was taking someone else to the prom. This didn't go over well with me. I decided that if I beat her, she wouldn't be able to go. As she was walking up the stairs one day, I hit her, but she didn't want to fight me. The rest of the day, I walked around the school with my belt buckle unfastened. This resulted in my being summoned to the front office. The police were waiting for me. They searched my pocketbook but didn't find anything. They talked to me, made me fasten my belt, and let me go back to class. My mother never found out about this incident.

The turmoil in our relationship went on for several months. Barry eventually became tired of this drama, and broke the relationship off. I thought permanently. As we walked home through the park one-day from school, with no fore warning, he shattered the limited stability that I had found my life.

He turned to me and said, "I love you Charlotte, but I'm not in love with you."

These words would remain with me for more years than I care to admit. They lingered in my mind, changing me inside out. There was no explanation; he refused to discuss his reasons for making the statement. My relationship with him at this time rather than building me up helped to tare me down. I blamed myself for the collapse of the relationship, feeling like a complete personal failure. He had been so cavalier about ending the relationship that I wanted to bury my feelings for him. I succeeded, burying the pain deep within my heart. Beneath the layers of my heart, the pain continued to erode my self-esteem.

We continued to see each other over the summer, almost on a daily basis. Daylight found us together, but at night he went another way. We went to summer school together that summer. After driving me to school, each day, his wall went up. There was no communication between us, until we were alone in the car. On the days when Barry wasn't able to drive us to school, my mother drove both of us to school. Barry wanted to finish school early, and go off to college in New Orleans in the fall. What I didn't know was that he was trying to get away from me. I was going to summer school to make up for the year that I had missed, after I was expelled from school because of my pregnancy.

Over the summer our relationship became stormier. The attraction was still strong between us, but I had never forgotten the words he had spoken to me in the park. He was afraid that I had no positive ambitions. At the time, he was right. He wanted to be a lawyer. The only thing I could think of was that I would be his secretary. His actions still said, "I love you." However, the words had done their damage, and I was moving even closer to hell. In August, he would leave for Xavier University, without clarifying our relationship. He was leaving me with a memory of walking though the park, a day when he shocked me with a declaration that seemed to fall from the trees. I would be left alone with my confusion, looking for someone else or something to fill the gap. In September, I would start the eleventh grade.

In the meantime, I became more and more convinced that I wanted to be treated like an adult. Trying to ease the pain and loneliness, I began mild experimentation with beer and marijuana, but I really didn't like either one of them. I was still trying to find a place to fit, to no avail. The gap between my mother and me was growing wider. Mama didn't know anything about drugs, but it was obvious to her that something was wrong with me. She tried to figure it out, but when she tried, she was wrong every time.

"You have been smoking marijuana."

This was on the day when I had been drinking. On the days when I had smoked marijuana, she got it wrong again.

"You're drunk! You've been drinking."

Most of the time, I didn't respond to her comments. Each day when I came home from school, I left Earline with my sister. Mama didn't like this. She wanted me to stay home with my baby. I wanted to numb my pain. Mama wanted me to be responsible. I was being responsible. Earline didn't need to be with me. One night when I was attempting to leave the house, Mama threatened to call the police if I left. This threat didn't go over well with me. She was bluffing and I called her bluff. After she refused to call the police, I called them. When the police arrived, Mama was crying, and I spoke to the policeman.

"This is my mother. She wanted to call you, because I won't stay at home."

Mama often said, "Two grown people can't live up under one roof. Somebody has to be the child."

She didn't mean this literally, and never planned for me to move out, but this made perfect sense to me. There was no way that I was going to act like a child. I moved in with Ma'Dear temporarily, for less than a couple of weeks. Almost immediately, I secured a job at a local cotton mill, working second shift. This was another mistake, because I sashayed into the mill each day directly from school, wearing my mini dresses, while everybody else arrived in their work clothes. This got me a lot of negative attention from both sexes, resentment from some women, and lust from some men. Within a month, at sixteen, I got my first apartment and moved out on my own. The rent was $65 a month. By lying about my age, I was able to secure credit at several furniture stores to furnish the apartment. Taking into consideration my age, I also asked Mama for financial support until my eighteenth birthday. She consented to my request.

By the time "Mr. Wright" returned home for his first visit, I had moved a little closer to hell. He had convinced me so that he didn't love me that I hadn't ever expected to see him again. Barry continued dropping by whenever he came to town, which wasn't often. In my mind, there was only one reason that he was coming by, to take advantage of my feelings for him. He wasn't telling me anything that made me think anything different. In fact, he seemed almost cold and indifferent. Each time, he returned, I had gotten closer to the pits of hell. He was also visiting my mother, and was very disturbed by what I was putting her through. Finally, he gave up and said that he wouldn't be coming back. I failed to equate any of this with my own actions, because all of conversations were presently tainted by our pride. We had perfected, "I don't care what you do." He would later tell me that it made him feel as if his life was out of control, each time he came to see me.

Barry became the plumb line for all my other relationships. Not that my other relationships had to measure up to him; it was that I lowered my expectations. I wasn't seeking emotional security, intellectual stimulation, spiritual stimulation, common goals, common interests, or a bright future. It was back to, "I just want someone to love me, for me." To further compound the issue, my conception of love had been extremely marred. Before Barry, I had always known when a relationship wasn't based on love. With him, I had been convinced for a season that there was a deep and abiding love between us. My concept of love was clouded by my breakup with Barry. My expectations of love had been extremely lowered.

Too many years, and too many pains later, he would tell me how much he had actually loved me, so much that he was risking achieving his professional goals. This is what caused him to break the relationship off. He said that when I moved out on my own, I moved toward a life style that he wanted to escape. We were finally able to put the pride aside and be honest with each other, but so many things had happened in the interim, our lives had taken different path, but oddly most of the good things overlapped. Interests that we never discussed were the same. When I think about Barry, there are a lot of "Ifs." If only you had... if only I had... if only I hadn't... if only you... if...

It became increasingly difficult to maintain a job from 3:00 p.m. until 11:00 p.m., and continue in school. Most of my time at school was spent sleeping. I had decided that I would never be able to attend college. My self-esteem had dropped so low that I was convinced I would never be able to pass the SAT. The GED began to seem more appealing to me, but I would need to be out of school for six months before being able to take the test. This sounded like a plan to me. One day, I was forced to leave school to change clothes. The counselor summoned me to the office; she told me that several girls had been overheard accusing their boyfriends of looking at my legs. She felt that it was best for me to change clothes to avoid being involved in a fight. One my instructors agreed to take me home to change, but my mind was made up, I wouldn't be going back.

My troubles at work were also increasing, as two men would make unwanted and unwarranted advances towards me. The first advance would result in my having to walk several miles home to avoid being raped. The first one had offered me a ride home from work. But rather than taking me home, he drove towards a wooded area on the other side of town. He told me that if I didn't sleep with him I would have to walk home. At 11:30 p.m., I jumped out of the car and started walking home. The time was well after midnight when I made it safely home.

The second man would show up on the doorstep of my apartment demanding that I open the door. He eventually left, after I refused to open the door. The next day at work, he found me in the break-room. There were several members of his family working at the mill including his wife and sister-in-law. We all worked the same shift. This didn't matter to him. He demanded to know why I hadn't opened the door. It didn't matter that his sister-in-law was listening. This set in motion a series of events that would cause his wife and me to be terminated the next day. She confronted me about her husband during the entire shift. We ended up fighting in the mill over a man that not even mosquitoes were interested in.

When we walked out of the mill that night, she had planned to ambush me. As I was getting into the car with one of my cousins, she touched me in the back with a wooden plank. When I turned around, she hit me across my right hand with a two by four. Somebody intervened after this to stop the attack. The next day my hand was treated at the infirmary, and we were summoned to the personnel office. When they told us that we were both being terminated, she begged them not to fire us, explaining that we had been friends. I sat there quietly, shocked by everything that had transpired. I was yet to figure out how her husband even knew where I lived. I was seventeen and knocking hard on hell's door.

Skin was in Germany, and he still hadn't seen my baby. Earline was almost two years old. We were writing sporadically, and sometimes I even called him but still, there was nothing that could be called a relationship. This was more of a diversion whenever I was lonely. It was getting close to time for him to return home on leave, and he promised that he would see the baby then.

One of my friends and I were walking down the street near my house one night, headed to a club. I still hadn't learned my lesson about hopping in cars with strangers. Two men pulled up beside us and asked if we wanted a ride. We were only going another block, but it was a nice car, so we decided to take the ride. She got in the back seat with one of the men and I got into the front seat with the driver.

The man that was driving asked me, "What's your name?"

I responded, "Charlotte."

He turned and looked me directly in my face, and said, "Charlotte, what?"

I responded, "Russell."

To my utter dismay he said, "I'm your Uncle Wallace."

I looked at him closely, and realized that he was telling the truth.

I told him, "You're a dirty old man let me out of this car."

He insisted that he knew who I was when he picked me up, but I didn't believe him. Although, I hadn't seen him in many years, this was indeed my uncle. My behavior never bothered him; we understood each other, "Black Sheep" to "Black Sheep." It seemed that my uncles were never really bothered by my behavior. This should have taught me a lesson about jumping into cars with strangers, but this didn't work.

THE DOOR OF HELL

His scales are his pride, shut up as with a

Job or no job, my mind was made up, I wasn't going. This was about the time that I met a man fifteen years older than I was. He was good looking, and this was what basically attracted me to him. We began to date, and shortly thereafter, he moved in with me. I had opened the door to hell. The relationship very quickly became extremely abusive. It wouldn't take long before he began abusing me physically and emotionally. He was obsessively jealous and in my confused mind, I thought this was love. I had no idea what love was or what I had gotten myself into. Robert Hall was a small man, about 5'5", less than 130 lbs. He was a man with an obvious Napoleon Complex. This is the "Small Man Complex" that causes a man who is small in statue to struggle to prove his manhood, usually by exerting power or authority over a person that he deems weaker or inferior.

The week that I met him, he taught me a lesson that I never forgot. That Friday when he got paid, he gave me a hundred-dollar bill. He left after this, going to a nearby club. Later that night, he returned asking me for two dollars. The only money that I had was what he had given me. I made the mistake of giving him the money. When he returned, he was broke and drunk. This was the last time that a man put money in my hands and got money back. Robert would continue to try this trick, but this never worked again. Whenever he put money in my hands, no matter what time of day or night, I went directly to the bank and deposited the money into my account.

Shortly after Robert moved in with me a pattern developed of him beating me, and me pressing charges, forcing him from the house. Early into my relationship with Robert, Skin returned home from Germany on leave. This was during one of the periods when Robert had beat me and moved out. Skin came by to see the baby, or maybe it wasn't the baby. Robert was staying in an apartment downstairs with his father. As Skin and I were sitting in the living room talking, Robert walked in and asked to see me in the bedroom. Once in the bedroom, he closed the door and beat me again. I'm not sure if Skin knew what was going on in the bedroom. When Robert was leaving the apartment, he told Skin not to say anything and walked out. I hadn't planned on letting Skin spend the night, but at the moment this didn't seem to matter.

The next day, Skin took my baby shopping and bought her an expensive dress, and a pair of gold earrings. He asked me if she needed else. This was a good gesture, but he acted like he had done thing spectacular. I told him that I had been doing a fine job of taking of my baby for almost two years by myself. She didn't need his charity. his was one of only three shopping trips that he ever took Earline on, during three trips home.

A few days later, I made the mistake of reconciling with Robert again. Something disastrous was about to happen in my life. We had a party at my house one night. Actually, this was a barbecue that kind of evolved into a party. My Uncle Carlton came. He was part of a group that kept going in and out of the bedroom doing drugs. During the 70s, a variety of drugs were popular, and a lot of teenagers were experimenting with them. I believe that this was TAC or some other hallucinogen, but I can't be sure.

Later that night, we went to the Mayfair Lounge. This was a block away from my apartment, which was located behind another club. As the evening wore on, Carlton became increasingly quiet. This really didn't bother me until we got ready to leave the club. Carlton wouldn't leave the club no matter I said or how hard I begged. He just sat there ignoring me. Realizing something was wrong, I had to call and tell our parents what was going on. Before they could get there to pick him up, Carlton left the nightclub walking towards Warren Williams. Our parents picked him up walking across the nearby railroad tracks.

The next morning, they called to tell me something was terribly wrong with Carlton. A short time later, he showed up at my apartment. He was wearing his brother's clothing which were three or four times too large for him. He was fluctuating between referring to himself as Teddy (his older brother) and the Pink Pimp. This was the scariest thing that had ever happened to me. I was afraid that my family would blame me for what had happened to him, but I had never seen or tried the drugs. Later, my uncle was admitted to West Central Georgia Regional Hospital for treatment. Tests would reveal that the drugs had caused brain damage. He would never be the same. This later happened to several of Carlton's friends. Carlton's condition finally stabilized with medication, but the damage was permanent.

At seventeen, I began working at the Mayfair Lounge. I wasn't old enough to sell alcoholic beverages but Robert worked this out with the manager. This lounge would lead me through the corridors of hell. While, I worked at the Mayfair, this also became my party ground when I wasn't working. I still hadn't developed a taste for alcohol, but I kept trying to get the hang of this. After all, I was involved with an alcoholic. Shortly after my eighteenth birthday, I married Robert Hall. This was my biggest mistake.

Not only was he an alcoholic and abusive, he was also extremely promiscuous. My mother begged me not to marry him. As usual, I wasn't going to listen to Mama.

While working at the Mayfair, I met a man who encouraged me to get my GED. In January 1978, I earned my GED and began attending technical college. Still without a clue what I wanted to do with my life, I enrolled in the Electronics Technology Program. An aptitude test revealed that I had the potential to complete the program, and the salary range for the field seemed appealing. During the first week of my classes, the instructors decided that I was too advanced academically for the classes, and decided to skip me to the second quarter classes. This was a mistake. I knew all of the information in the first half of the textbooks, but there were things in the back of the book that I needed to learn before going to the second quarter classes. In spite of the problems in my relationship with Robert, I managed to complete one quarter of the program. By the next quarter, my life would move in a different direction, and to a different city.

The relationship with Robert could only be characterized as a series of hurricanes. The beatings were often public, to include several at the Mayfair. In his drunken stupor, he would often give me a pistol. He said I was to use the gun to protect myself. The only problem was that he was the only person that I needed protection from. During one of our many separations, Robert came to the Mayfair, intent on causing another scene. I was working that night. He sat there all night getting drunk and watching me. The drunker he got the crazier and more belligerent he became. He began to threaten me, and finally followed me into the women's bathroom. Several men pulled him out of the bathroom.

He said, "I just want to give her something."

He handed me a loaded gun. I took the gun from his hand, wondering if he had actually planned to shoot me, if these men hadn't intervened. I felt safer with the gun in my possession. One man agreed to walk me home after the club closed.

Several days later, Robert moved back into the apartment with me again. He wanted me to give the gun back to him, but I was afraid to give it back. One day while he was in the bathtub bathing, he was also screaming obscenities and intimidation at me.

Demanding he said, "When I get out of the bathtub, you better have the gun."

I walked to the kitchen and removed the loaded gun from the oven. When I returned to the bedroom, I sat crossed legged on the bed, waiting for him to get out of the bathtub. He walked out of the bathroom and into the bedroom wrapped only in a towel, unprepared for what he saw. Pointing the gun directly at him, I gave him instructions.

"Pickup the telephone and call the police."

He refused to make the call, choosing to take the gun from me. When he reached for the, gun, I pulled the trigger. This was the first time that I fired a pistol and my arm jerked. The bullet went about an inch above his head. The bullet traveled through the wall in my room and lodged somewhere in the wall of my daughter's room. No one was hurt, but, instantly, he was willing to call the police. He finished getting dressed, while we were both waiting for their arrival. When the policeman arrived, I was sitting in the same place, on the bed, holding the gun. He told the policeman that he didn't want to press charges against me. He just wanted me to give him the gun. The policeman confiscated the gun and forced him to leave the apartment. No charges were filed.

It wouldn't be long before he returned to the apartment, and the pattern repeated again. Somehow, the power he exuded over me made him feel like a man. I was afraid of him but I wasn't prone to letting him get away with hurting me. After one of the beatings, he decided that he would make sure that I couldn't leave the house. He sat on the living room sofa blocking the only exit from the apartment, the front door. The apartment was on the top level of a two-story building, making leaving through a window impossible. Knowing that he would eventually succumb to the alcohol, I waited for him to fall asleep. When he dozed off, my plan was put in motion. My pocketbook and my guitar were placed next to the door for my escape, while being careful not to awaken him. Then, I tipped into the bathroom for a can of shaving cream, and began squeezing the cream into the palms of my hands. With my hands full of shaving cream, I tipped back to the sofa where Robert was sleeping. Almost with one motion, I put all the shaving cream in his face and began beating him over the head, as hard as I could with the guitar. He tried to rub the cream from his eyes, but there was too much foam. The shaving cream caused him to be blinded temporarily, long enough for me to get away. As he was trying to recover, I grabbed my pocketbook and ran all the way to Warren Williams.

Robert was constantly looking for a new woman to have a relationship with. Sometimes, he would be gone from home for the entire weekend. When he made one of these trips, my decision was made to get even with him. My sister-in law had told me about burning some of her boyfriend's clothing and placing the ashes on his wife's doorstep. This gave me an idea. There was a big barrel grill downstairs outside of his father's apartment. After bundling everything that Robert owned together in piles, I began taking them downstairs to the grill. After assuring that nothing remained in the house, I got the lighter fluid and matches. All the items in the grill were doused with the lighter fluid and started the fire. This was like a big bonfire. The fire flamed higher than was intended and the heat awakened his father. The grill was next to his father's bedroom window. His father watched from the window but didn't say anything. He had never liked me and this wasn't going to make things better. Thankfully, the whole apartment building wasn't burned down, but everything that he owned with the exception of the items that he had taken with him was burned.

The police would be called on a continuous basis throughout the relationship. There would be several attempts to kill him in response to the beatings. Later, we moved to a better apartment downtown, on Broadway. Things really got out of hand one day, when he attempted to beat me in the presence of our family and friends. I was able to make it to my car with my cousin and my baby. He walked towards me screaming obscenities, and threw a set of keys at the car. Determined to end the abuse, I placed my foot on the accelerator and pressed the pedal to the floor. At the last minute, he realized the car was going to hit him and jumped to the side of the street. Putting the car in reverse, I backed up the street. He ran onto the sidewalk. Not to be deterred, I drove the car up on the sidewalk. This time Robert was hit with the car. Afterwards the car swerved and hit a sign in front of a house located next to our apartment building. While he was lying on the ground, I attempted to no avail to crank the car. I wanted to finish what had been started. Earline was in the back seat, with an ice chest directly behind her head.

Irritated, Earline said, "Look what you did to me."

Frantic, I looked back, scared that I had hurt my child in my anger. She wasn't hurt; ice had wasted all over her clothes.

There were two people watching this scene that chose to risk intervening. A friend of Robert's picked him up from the ground and got him to the hospital. One of my neighbors in the apartment complex took me into her home and attempted to calm me down. We had never met before this incident, but she was willing to chance getting involved.

"Come on and get out of the car. You can stay at my house until you calm down."

Disappointed that I hadn't finished him off, I went with her. This was the day that my cousin learned to drive. Apparently, Sonya figured it was safer for her to drive than it was for me. There was nothing wrong with the car or my passengers, and the car needed to be moved from the sidewalk. The keys had been left in the car. Sonya drove the car from the sidewalk and around the building. Knowing there would be a problem when he was released from the hospital, I decided to leave almost everything that I owned and moved to Atlanta, GA. My journey was taking me down another corridor in hell.

While working at the Mayfair, I met a pimp who was also a drug dealer, Jim (not his real name), who lived in Atlanta. He was my biggest tipper, whenever he was in town. Often, he would buy drinks for everyone in the nightclub. Liking his generosity, or his ability to flaunt his money, I would tease him.

"If I ever decide to work the streets, I am going to find you."

This wasn't my intention in leaving Columbus, but upon my arrival in Atlanta, I was broke and my car needed minor repairs, unrelated to my hitting Robert. There was one person in the city that I knew who would be willing to get the car repaired. This would also provide an opportunity to have some fun. It was thus that my ignorance took me down to Peachtree Street looking for Jim.

When we got to Atlanta, we moved in with my Aunt Bobbie, Sonya's mother. I knew that Jim could be found on Peachtree Street or Auburn Avenue. It would be easy to figure out which end of the streets. Both streets had sections where there was high level of illegal activities. All we had to do was look for signs of trouble. Sonya rode the bus everywhere that she traveled, and whenever we went anywhere she took me the bus route. This helped me to learn my way around Atlanta. All we had to do to find Jim was watch the people when we traveled down the streets. We would know when we reached the stroll. I found Jim with very little effort on Peachtree Street, and he gave me the money to get my car repaired. Once I located Jim, I took Sonya to her boyfriend's house, a short distance away, and went back to hang out with Jim on Peachtree.

In those days there was no king in Israel: every man did what was right in his own eyes. Judges 21:25

Peachtree Street was full of activity from one end of the street to the other. The street actually ran across a very large section of Atlanta, but this was unknown to me at the time. We had started our search at the end of the street that was closest to Auburn Avenue. This enabled us to find our destination rather quickly. In this section of Peachtree both drugs and women were abundantly available if you had the money. One street over, men were abundantly available if you had enough money. If you didn't make careful observation, you might get confused. A few blocks from the parking lot where I would be hanging out, bathhouses and strip joints lined the blocks. During the day the street took on the scene of a boring business district, with only minor indications of the way the street came alive at night. If you looked closely during the day, you would see an occasional hooker. The night crowd went in about 7:00 a.m., and returned after dark when the legitimate businesses closed. This was when everything and everybody came out.

Each night Sonya and I began a regular routine of leaving the house together but heading to two different destinations. We left Earline with Aunt Bobbie each night. Sonya and I would plan a time for me to pick her back up. Sometimes, she would decide she wasn't ready to go home. On these nights or mornings, I would go to Aunt Carrie's to avoid answering questions about where Sonya had been left. I wouldn't go back without Sonya. Aunt Bobbie had to be at work by 7:00 a.m. Sometimes, we didn't get there until 6:30 a.m. or later. Even though, I had been up all night, my aunt made me take her to work. This was dangerous, because I was falling asleep most of the way, and running off the street. Every time we stopped at a red light or behind a bus I went to sleep.

Earline and Aunt Bobbie were good friends; they were "Beer Buddies." Earline was only suppose to get a sip of the beer, but this wasn't how it worked out most of the time. Once when we were coming to Columbus, Earline and Aunt Bobbie were sitting in the back seat of the car. Aunt Bobbie had her beer as usual. Earline was drinking with her. Earline was instructed several times to stop drinking the beer.

She responded, "I'm never going to stop drinking beer."

She didn't stop that day, knowing that Ma'Dear would never let me hit her. Soon, she would be safe in Columbus. The declaration that Earline had made was far from the truth.

And she shall follow after her lovers, but she shall not overtake them; and she shall seek them and shall not find them: then she shall say, I will go and return to my first husband; for then was it better with me than now. Hosea 2:7

A few days after my first trip to Peachtree Street, I began selling drugs on the Ho-stroll. This would begin a pattern that continued for a number of years. When there was no safety or security in my marriage, I would revert to the streets where a different type of security was found. There was no physical, verbal, or emotional abuse for me on the streets. Jim was usually occupied somewhere else with someone else. He made sure there was someone looking out for my safety. There were no demands or pressures from him. Jim and I seldom spent time together and this worked for both of us. He spent just enough time with me to make sure that I didn't leave him. This wasn't the way that I had planned this, but street life was still safer than my marriage.

Peggy and Charlotte

STREET LIFE

And they consider not in their hearts that I remember all their wickedness: now their own doings have beset them about; they are before my face.

Immediately, Jim introduced me to Liz to facilitate my drug business on Peachtree. They had been friends for along time and she could really sling dope. Liz was a heroin addict and as such couldn't be trusted to hold a package. She understood this and was willing to work with me. Liz was also several months pregnant. We sold drugs until early each morning, usually going in about 10:00 a.m. Often Liz would crash at my room.

When her pregnancy advanced, she continued to abuse intravenous drugs. After the labor pains began, Liz used drugs to stop the pains. Finally, the pains stopped completely. She knew that once she got to the hospital, there would be a lot of questions, and she would have several days before she could get high again. After she had put off going to the hospital for two days, I insisted on dropping her off at the hospital. Not wanting to be tied to the drugs that were sure to be found in her system, I didn't go in with her. Later that day, I went back to check on her. The baby boy was born addicted to Heroin. After checking on Liz, I walked down to the nursery to check on the baby. There were tubes attached to his head, and they were attempting to extract the drugs from his system. There would be several days before Liz was released from the hospital, and even longer before the baby would be well enough to be released.

Momentarily, with Liz in the hospital, I needed to come up with another way to peddle the drugs. While on Peachtree, I had observed the patterns of the people on the stroll. Most of the girls were IV drug users. Most of them were trying to hide this from their pimps. If they were caught using drugs they would be beaten. The pimps had certain times that they checked their traps (checked with their women to pick up the money). Timing the pimps' rounds would enable me to ride through and check their traps before they did. When I swung my car door open, the girls would jump in and lay down in the floor, one on top of the other, packed like sardines in a can. Then I would take them somewhere that they could get off. There was a gas station on Peachtree that was particularly handy for this purpose. If they had enough money, the ride took them across town. They were sold a large quantity of drugs before my trip back to Peachtree.

It wasn't long before the pimps figured out what was going on. All of the girls were restricted from riding with me. One night, Susan was taken to the gas station to get off. Her man, Slick got wind of what was going on. He tracked us down at the gas station. Just when Susan was about to take her hit, Slick's arm came smashing through the window on the door of the women's bathroom. Quickly, my escape was made back to my car, not wanting to be there if the police came. He was still beating her when I sped off. The next time I saw him, a cast covered most of his arm.

When Liz was released from the hospital, she caught a cab back to Peachtree looking for a hit. The baby remained in the hospital for several months. We didn't hang together much any more. I now knew most of the people on the stroll who got high. My new way of hustling was worked better financially for me, and the profits wouldn't have to be shared with her. Immediately after being released from the hospital, she began getting high again. Eventually, she disappeared off the scene. I never saw her or the baby again.

Rumors about my escapades on Peachtree Street begin to fly with the wind, and they flew all the way back to Columbus. And as usual, in the absence of fact, family fire would make up the details. My family in Columbus would be extremely disturbed by the reports of what I was doing on Peachtree Street. By this time I had gotten accustomed to being lied on. There was no need to justify my behavior. Amidst all of the complaints about my behavior, no one was offering to provide me the financial security that was needed. My grandmother would send my aunt and uncle to Atlanta with an empty suitcase and instructions. Knowing that I wouldn't defy her instructions, they were told to pack my daughter's belongings and bring her back to Columbus. This was ideal for me since I was living in hotels, and didn't want my daughter exposed to Peachtree Street or the drug environment. This would also eliminate a need to see my family in Atlanta regularly. I thought this would solve my problems with family fire, but I was mistaken.

Tired of living in hotels, I began to pester Jim to secure me a permanent place to reside. He kept putting this off, so I decided to handle things myself. Without him knowing it, I rented an apartment in Atlanta. Then I returned to Columbus to pickup my furniture and clothing. My plans were to pick my belongings up while Robert was at work. However, upon my arrival, the lock on the door of the apartment had been changed. It would be necessary for me to see him to get my things. This didn't scare me. I knew that he would be missing me.

Therefore pride compasseth them about as a chain; violence covereth them as a garment. Psalm 73:6

After leaving the apartment complex, I saw my other car parked in a neighboring apartment complex. Very calmly, I pulled up behind the car. Robert and his mother were in the car, but his new girlfriend was driving the car. His mother jumped out of the car, speaking a warning to the woman behind the steering wheel.

She said, "Chauna is going to get you about her husband."

His mother was never able master the pronunciation of my name. It was obvious that Robert was glad to see me, therefore, I just told him where he would be able to find me later. He was on his way to work at a nearby restaurant. His girlfriend dropped him off at work, but he went in the front door and out the back door, immediately after she pulled off. Within the hour he had walked several blocks to meet me. My pride was going to cause me another problem, since I was determined to show her that she couldn't take my husband. To my detriment, my point was proved.

We left town together for several days. When we returned to Columbus we discovered that the other car had been totaled in a wreck. After realizing Robert had left town with me, his girlfriend became extremely upset. Crying as she drove through the historic district of Columbus, she ran the car off the street. The car stopped on the steps of a house sitting back from the streets. The frame of the car was bent. When we got to the apartment, she had moved all of her belongings. My point was proven, but I was making a big mistake; my husband went back to Atlanta with me. The cycle would begin again, the honeymoon, alcohol, women, beatings, and me leaving.

During the times that Robert and I were living together, there was no need for me to sell drugs. Actually, he wouldn't have allowed me to sell drugs. Although, he was always doing his own thing, he tried to monitor my actions closely. I worked as a waitress at various restaurants in the Atlanta area. Robert was able to land some good jobs immediately. The problem was that he spent most of his money buying alcohol, and lost whatever he had left. Whatever money he was going to provide to take care of the house had to come off the top. He was very generous if I got to him before he started drinking. Within a few months, we were able to move to a better apartment.

Searching for peace within, I began to read the Bible for consolation. This resulted in beatings, too. There was only one Bible in the house, one that Robert had been given by his daughter (from a previous marriage). He never read the Bible, and didn't want me to read it. When he wasn't home, I would read the Bible and call my Aunt Bobbie to discuss what I was reading. One day while I was talking to her over the telephone, Robert returned home. The Bible was in my hand. He immediately snatched the Bible from my hand, and began beating me. This Bible wasn't meant to be read. This one was only to be used for ornamentation.

Financially, things were going well, but the adultery and abuse continued. Eventually, I would get tired of the pattern. During one of his all night escapades, I packed my clothes, and hid them in the closet near the front entrance to the apartment. When he returned the next day, he asked for my set of keys to the car. Knowing that he had been drinking the night before, I convinced him that he had lost the keys during his outing. He insisted that I accompany him to look for the keys. At each stop, he would carefully ensure that I couldn't drive off. Finally, he became relaxed, leaving the car running, as he went into one of his friend's house. I slipped into the driver's seat, quickly returned to the apartment for my clothes. After making a quick stop by the hotel where I was working to pick up my paycheck, with my daughter, I returned to Columbus. There was just one problem; I had only a limited amount of money. This wasn't enough money to hold me more than a week, and we needed a place to stay.

Immediately, I would find out my other friend, Jim, had also moved back to Columbus. After explaining to him what had happened with Robert, he gave me a pistol in a pouch. He laid the pouch on the table in the Mayfair. This marked the period that I began carrying a gun to protect myself from further beatings. There was never a need for me to use this gun, but my mind was made up, the gun would be used if needed. My intentions were that if it became necessary for me to use this gun, I would shoot to kill. This would prevent the perpetrator from retaliating. This was a lesson that one of my uncles had taught me. He told me that it was dangerous to beat someone and then turn your back, allowing them time to recover and retaliate.

Also, during this time, my bad habits were brought to the streets of Columbus. In an effort to respect my mother, I saw her as seldom as possible. I kept most of my clothes in the car, and only dropped by when I needed to swap clothes. My mother would allow me to stay with her, but not on my own terms. Therefore, this was just a place to park my clothes. My daughter and I spent most of our time in the East Wynnton neighborhood. A large portion of the neighborhood is highly infected with heavy drug traffic. Most of my time would be spent on a street that only spanned two blocks. One-bedroom brick apartments on both sides of the streets lined one of the blocks. This is the block where most of my time was spent, peddling drugs.

Immediately, I began clubbing every night, going from one club to another. Jim was frequenting these same clubs. His friends would ask him, how could I work the streets if I was in the clubs all the time. Trying to maintain his image, he would tell me to leave and go to work, making sure that they overheard him. Knowing this was a pride thing with him, I would merely say, "Okay." I would leave that club and go to another one on the next block. Later when Jim showed up at that club, I would say, "I'm leaving." This was our normal way of relating. No one knew that this was an unspoken understanding between us. As long as I didn't disrespect him, I did whatever I wanted to. Most of the time my comments were very polite. Sometimes, he made me mad and that other side came out.

This was during this time that I met Mr. Chuck, Jim's father. He would become my friend, surrogate father, encourager, baby-sitter, and bondsman. There wasn't a period of getting aquatinted. For some reason, he just liked me. Chuck didn't approve of my relationship with his son.

He would constantly say, "Don't be a fool. That nigga is low down."

Of course, I didn't listen to him. This wouldn't stop him from bailing me out when I got in trouble. There would be plenty of these opportunities, since trouble seemed to find me.

When Jim arrived in Columbus, he brought with him a young son and daughter by a previous marriage, and Cathy, one of his women. My daughter and his children were very close in age. Earline, my daughter was four. Lil' Jim was three, and Selene was five. Cathy usually kept the children during the day. This was normally when I worked selling drugs.

Chuck would keep the children at night, while we were in the streets. This was normally at my request. He would make me promise to come back at a decent hour. I returned at whatever time he requested, but I had a strange way of doing it. If he told me to come back by 12:00, this is exactly what I would do. At 12:00, I would ride past his house to see if the lights in his house were on. If the lights were on or the television, I would keep riding pass the apartment. Later on, I would ride through again. This pattern continued until I was sure all the lights were out, signaling that he had put the children to bed. Then and only then would I park the car and get out. Making sure that the neighbors saw me, I eased to the door and softly tapped. I was extremely careful not to wake Chuck or the children. After this, I hurried back to the car, and back to the clubs. When I finally returned later in the morning, I would assure Chuck that I had made every effort to pick up the children. He knew I was lying, but he never got mad with me.

Jim had a way of ensuring that the people in the neighborhood wouldn't turn on him. Often, he provided money for groups of neighborhood children to go to the movies. On more than one occasion, he sponsored barbecues and invited everybody in the neighborhood. He purchased all the food and alcohol. The full buffet consisted of ribs, chicken, steaks, potato salad, collard greens, black-eyed peas, macaroni and cheese, baked beans, and a variety pies and cakes. There was also an alcohol buffet, with an even larger selection. However, he disappeared after providing the money to purchase everything, leaving his sister, Reba and me to do all the cooking. This was part of his flamboyant style that originally caught my attention.

Jim had Cathy working Victory Drive. Occasionally, I would ride through there to see if anything was happening. This happened approximately twice a month (soldiers' payday), and then my way made to the clubs. If Jim asked what happened, I merely responded that nothing was happening. He accepted this from me, because this had never been his idea for me to go out there the first time. Cathy wasn't allowed this privilege, and she told me how bad she wanted to be able to go to the clubs. I began plotting to grant her wish. The opportunity arrived one day, when Jim had to go back to Atlanta to pick up another package of drugs.

While he was gone, I was supposed to sell the remaining drugs. Cathy was supposed to work Victory Drive. This was the time to put the plan into action. When Cathy brought me the children, I swapped cars with her and also kept the key to her house. This would give Cathy an excuse to come to the Mayfair later on that night. I made arrangements for Chuck to baby-sit the kids, my daughter and Jim's two kids by his ex-wife. Confident that Jim would never hit me, I planned to take responsibility for the events of the evening.

When Cathy arrived at the Mayfair, the coast was clear, since Jim hadn't arrived back from Atlanta. Deciding to give her a long night out, I told her to follow me to the H&D in the neighboring city (a club in Phenix City, Alabama) that would be open until about 6:00 a.m. This was part of my normal routine. Telling Cathy that it was best for her to keep her money, I agreed to buy everything that she wanted with the money made from the drug transactions. Like a bird finally released from its cage, Cathy took this night further than what had been planned. After getting sloppy drunk, she began to dance with several of Jim's friends. As the club closed, she tried to leave with one of them. I insisted that she ride back with me, grabbing her by the arm and putting her into Jim's car. One of my friends drove the other car back to Jim's father house.

As we drove back to Columbus, Cathy began to get scared that Jim was back from Atlanta. She was drunk and sick on the stomach. Sure that I could handle this situation, I gave her instructions to let me do all the talking. When both cars pulled up in front of Chuck's house, Jim was standing in the yard obviously angry. When Jim questioned where we had been, my plan went out the window when the alcohol that Cathy had consumed began to talk. As she responded, I stopped and stood by the car. My friends went across the street and waited.

"You go every _____ night. Why can't we go?"

She staggered up the steps to Chuck's house without ever looking back. Jim was running briskly behind her. Grabbing her from behind, he pulled her down the steps and began beating her. I waited behind the safety of the car, no longer sure that he wouldn't hit me. After he finished beating Cathy, he demanded that I come to him.

I responded, "I don't think so."

He ran towards me as fast as he could. Standing by the car proved to be a wise choice. After chasing me around the car a few times, he got tired. He walked to the corner screaming obscenities. This gave me a chance to run inside Chuck's house and lock the front door. Chuck told me that he had to let his son in, but he wouldn't let him hit me. I tried to make it out the back door, but I was too nervous to get the door open. For Cathy's benefit, he told me that he would get me the next day. This didn't worry me; I knew I had gotten away without the beating. Somehow I think he understood that I had enough beatings, and if he began this practice it would destroy my reasons for running from my marriage to him.

While in Atlanta, I had been arrested a few times on misdemeanor violations for which I would be released within the hour. When I was eighteen, I had been arrested once on a felony charge of burglary. I was accused of breaking into one of my neighbor's house and stealing an old rabbit coat. Robert had actually found the coat outdoors. This neighbor's husband had a special place that he preferred to park. Robert parked in this parking place. The man came to the door of our apartment and demanded that Robert move my car. Robert went out to move the car, but when Robert got smart with him, he beat Robert to a pulp. The next day, Robert found the coat in the parking lot where the man had beat him. He gave me the coat. Since I didn't want the coat, I tried to sell the coat to one of our neighbors. This neighbor knew who was the owner of the coat, and immediately told the owner. Rather than asking for the coat, after she discovered who had found the coat, and still angry about the dispute between her husband and Robert, she accused me of breaking into her house.

There was no question of my innocence of this charge. The person making the charge had a long history of shoplifting. The arresting officers stated to me that they knew that I was innocent. However, the y also stated that I stayed in a high crime neighborhood, and they needed information on several burglaries in the downtown area. They told me they only helped people who helped them. There was nothing I could do to help them, and they did nothing to help me. I spent the night in a dark, damp, cold, and filthy cell. The bars opened to the hall. There was a commode in the cell but nothing to shield it from anyone walking down the hall, and there was no toilet tissue. A metal frame served as a bed, without a mattress. The tears that I shed all night made the cell colder and my bed harder. For breakfast the next morning, they served a hard ugly biscuit and fried fat back that I refused to eat. That night, I vowed to myself that if I ever went back to jail, I would be guilty. With one exception, I would keep this vow.

My mother hired a lawyer to represent me on these charges. I was indicted by the Grand Jury but the case was never brought to court. During the time that I had lived in Atlanta, I tried to get the case brought to court or disposed of. I didn't want this hanging over my head indefinitely. Somehow, when my lawyer checked on disposing the case, there was no record of my having been arrested on the charge.

Oh, back to this stupid vow that I made to myself. Now that I was back in Columbus, I would get arrested for a series of misdemeanor violations. Usually, Mr. Chuck would bail me out within a few hours. The most serious charge again was one where I was innocent. A policeman accused me of trying to run him over, and thus charged me with aggravated assault on a police officer. What this really amounted to was that he had tried to no avail to flag me down to give me a trespassing charge, as I was riding around a motel on Victory Drive. When I pulled into the parking lot of the motel, two policemen were standing in front of the motel. I drove around the motel and exited the parking lot on the other side of the motel. When I returned to an adjoining restaurant a few weeks later, one of the policemen arrested me, claiming that I had tried to run him over the last time that I had been in the area. However, I never saw him trying to flag me down. He was actually standing in the breezeway of the hotel when I passed by. At least, I didn't have anything illegal on me.

After moving back to Columbus, I began to try to establish a relationship with one of my grandmothers. From time to time I would take her to pay bills or to the grocery store. One day when I was taking her home, I hit another car at an intersection of two roads. The driver of the other car was taking supplies to a function at his church. There was someone else following behind him in another car headed to the church. Rushing to get the supplies to the church, he left his car in the road and jumped into the second car. I had a package of cocaine (a package consisting of several individual dosages) on me, and decided that I needed to call Jim. Not only was I carrying the cocaine, I had the pistol and I was driving his car without the proper documentation. Jim told me to hide the drugs and the gun, and he would come to pick them up. After doing this, I realized I had a perfect opportunity to get away. There was one problem, my grandmother refused to get back in the car. She was only a couple of blocks from her house, so I left her waiting for the police. When they arrived, she gave them my name and my mother's address.

Meanwhile, I went to exchange Jim's car with my own car. I needed to hide Jim's car. My car was at my mother's house. The tags on the cars had been swapped, because the finance company was looking for his car. My younger sister, Crystal, didn't know how to drive but on this day she would have to quickly learn. She was about sixteen at the time. I gave her quick instructions.

"This is the brake and this is the gas. When you see my brake light come on put your foot on the brake. This is the signal. When I put my signal on you put yours on. Trust me and stay close to me."

She followed me across town to hide Jim's car. I swapped the tags back on the cars so that my car would have the correct tag. This went off without a hitch. By the time I arrived back at my mother's house to drop Crystal off, the police had already been there looking for me. I called a bondsman and asked him to meet me at the jail, and then I went to turn myself in at the jail.

After I was released from jail, Jim had a surprise for me. There had only been about three hours since I had hid the dope. He told me that he found the gun but that he couldn't find the drugs that I hid. He asked me to go back and look for the drugs. Even though I knew that he was lying, I went through the process of searching for the drugs that I had hid. There were no drugs to be found. Of course, he had already found the drugs. I knew this when he sent me back to the site of the accident. This was an excuse for him not to pay his supplier for the drugs.

This was around the time that Jim decided he was going to New York City, for awhile. He was going by himself, leaving Cathy and me behind. He was also leaving Lil' Jim and Selene behind with their mother, who had recently moved to Columbus. I had a court date pending; therefore, I told him I would join him after I paid my fines. This was my idea and I don't think he really believed me. Again, Mr. Chuck warned me not to be a fool, but he also told me that if Jim mistreated me, he would send for me. That Friday, I paid my fines, and began making plans to travel to New York. Saturday morning, I caught a ride to Atlanta with my cousin who was headed that way. I left my daughter with my mother. This wasn't a problem, since Mama wasn't happy about me going, let alone my taking Earline.

The court fines had been more than I expected and I had only about $20 dollars when I arrived in Atlanta. This didn't seem like a big problem for me. I dropped my bags off with another cousin and caught a cab to Peachtree Street. On Peachtree Street, I saw Jim's brother and told him where I was headed. He told me that I had so much nerve that if I didn't have all the money that I needed by the end of the night, he would give me the difference. From the telephone booth, we called a bar in Harlem to tell Jim that I would be coming in on the "Early-Bird Flight." This flight was cheaper than the other flights. At the end of the evening, I had just enough money for the flight. Not having any money to spare, I caught a ride to the airport.

I arrived at the airport about fifteen minutes after the plane left the airport. I would need to take a later plane, and I was $30 short on my fare. Not to be deterred, I introduced myself to a porter, explained my situation, and asked for the $30. I had noticed him looking at me. Not only did he give me the additional funds that I needed, he gave me some advice.

"If there is any problem when you reach the airport in New York, find another porter. He'll be happy to assist you."

I responded, "Thank you, Sir."

Happy to have overcome this hurdle, I didn't think about the next one. I thought I had everything under control, once I purchased my ticket. If I could overcome my fear of taking my first airplane flight, I would be fine. Choosing to sit in an aisle seat on the plane, I was careful not to look out the window. As we neared the airport, I thought it was a shame that I wasting the opportunity to observe the scenery from the plane. I decided to take a quick glance. The flashing glance was really beautiful, but I quickly turned away again. Although, there were no problems on the flight, I exited from the plane with my fear of flying in tact.

Arriving in New York City about 9:00 a.m. on a Sunday morning with only the number to a bar and a dime for the telephone call, I had a bigger problem. As I dialed the number, there was no answer at the bar. Finally, it dawned on me that due to the time delay the bar was closed. Looking around, I found a porter who was going off duty. He was also a taxi driver. Again, I explained my situation. He told me that he would do whatever he could to help me, but he was afraid to take me to Harlem. He told me that if I would agree to date him, he would give me some money, and take me to the outskirts of Harlem. Additionally, he explained that due to his age he would need special attention to complete the act.

I responded, "No sir, I'm sorry I don't do that."

He responded, "I can't believe you're this far from home, and without any money, and you can still say what you don't do."

Again, I responded, "Sir I'm sorry, but I can't do that."

I didn't know what I was going to do, but that wasn't an option. I never had, and I wasn't about to now. Confident that something else would work out, I held my ground. Reluctantly, he agreed to take me within a few blocks of my destination. However, on the way, he told me that I had too much nerve that he felt bad about being scared to take me to Harlem. He drove me to my destination and gave me $50. Jim was standing outside of a hotel next to the bar, as I exited the cab. There was a look of disbelief on his face that quickly turned into a broad smile. Thus, I made my trip to Harlem.

And they considered not in their hearts that I remember all their wickedness: now their own doings have beset them about; they are before my face. Hosea 7:2

The hotel where we would stay was more like a huge rooming house, with three floors. There was a stoop marking the entrance to the hotel. The man that ran the hotel lived on the lower floor. He was the first person that I needed to become friends with. The stoop would later become where I sat to peddle my drugs. This was next door to the bar that I had tried to call that morning. On the other side of the bar was a church. All along both sides of the street there were people standing around, most involved in some type of illegal drug activity. Most of the people that regularly peddled drugs on this block were from Columbus or Durham, North Carolina. People were pushing racks of clothes and carts loaded with other goods down the street selling them. You could buy anything that you needed by just standing outside on this block. Within two blocks, you could find any type of drug that you wanted. This wasn't hidden activity. This was an

58

excepted practice in this area. Dealers walked up and down the street all day and all night singing.

"Tees, Blues, Specks, Sparklers, Beauties, Whites, Pinks, Purples…"

I would make several trips each day to pick up my marijuana. About two blocks away, there was a hole where I went to get the drugs. This was a literal hole. You walked down two steps, up to the hole in the wall. You either said red (for Panama Red), gold (for Panama gold), or black (for Pakistani black) to identify the kind of marijuana that you wanted. A hand would extend from the wall to take the money and then give you the kind of marijuana that you had requested. There was marijuana from all over the world. There was Zambia, Thai sticks from Thailand (bundles of marijuana soaked in hashish oil or marijuana buds bound on short sections of bamboo), Sinsemilla (a potent variety marijuana) Colombian Gold, Mexican brown, Mexican red, Black gunion, African black, Acapulco gold and opium to name only a few of the drugs. This was like a wholesale outlet that sold only drugs.

I had heard about what were called "New York Junkies," but nothing prepared me for what I saw. Junkies in Georgia couldn't touch this. There were men and women whose arms and legs were swollen three or four times their normal proportions, a result of intravenous drug usage. Their hands were referred to as baseball mitts. Covering their skin was not just tracks (marks identifying the points that intravenous drugs had entered their body), but often sores that were oozing with infectious puss. For a small amount of drugs you get them to run drugs for you all day, since they never seemed to sleep. You could only give them a sack of dope at a time. After they made several transactions for you, then you gave them something for personal usage.

The best food was found in two places. The first was the church that was located next to the bar. Sometimes, they sold dinners at the church. This was the closest that you came to Southern cooking. Whenever they sold dinners, you had to rush to get one before they sold out. Some cooks were better than others were, but this was worth the risk to get one of the good ones. The other place to get good food was several blocks away, "Wells." You had to catch a taxi to get to Wells, but this was worth it to get fried chicken breast and waffles.

Immediately after arriving in the city, I would find someone to supply my three basic needs, food, shelter, and marijuana. All I had to do to accomplish this was find a man with that look of lust in his eyes. There would be no need for sexual relationships with these men. The hope that someday there would be something in return would go along way. There was one person for food and marijuana and another for shelter and marijuana. I was crazy enough to follow Jim but not crazy enough to trust him. Within days, I would be working the streets of New York. There were difficult days, however, making the transition to the city. There were still things that I refused to do even if I was hungry. Jim understood this, and never pushed me to change my principles. Many days in the beginning, Jim and I would split $5 for the day's meal. Somehow, this made us closer, and he actually treated me better away from home. During the months in New York, I would call Chuck each Sunday to let him know how I was being treated.

I forgot to mention that one of the reasons for Jim changing cities regularly was this bad habit he had of not paying people for their dope. He would get these packages on credit. Sometimes these packages were already packaged for resale, and other times they had to be broken down in smaller quantities. Anytime the dope was high quality (extremely potent), he was going to open the package and add a stretcher to the drugs. He would also sell the high quality dope to get things kicked off, and then he would recut the dope lessening the quality of the dope. Usually, he would pay the person that had gotten the dope from all of the money, for the first couple of times. After he had gained their confidence, he would increase the depth of his debt. Normally, he was working on getting over on several people at a time. When his debt increased to a significant amount, he would disappear to a new city. After a significant time passed, he would return.

True to form, in New York City, he would recut each package that he received. He would add additional additives to the drugs, lessening the quality of the drugs to increase his profits. I would sit on the stoop of the hotel where we stayed in Harlem and peddle the drugs. Almost like clockwork, one night he would call and tell me that I needed to move out of the hotel in Harlem, and move downtown the next morning. This didn't suit my plan. Everything that I needed was in Harlem, and this is where I planned on staying. Jim didn't tell me why he was moving, but I would find out the next day.

When I walked out of the hotel the next morning, it seemed that everybody was looking for Jim. He had left owing several people for drugs. They wanted me to tell them how to find him, but that wasn't going to happen. I had no intention of calling him for anybody including myself. However, there was one person who knew that I had the answer to his whereabouts. He wasn't going to be deterred easily, and I knew enough about him to know that he was serious. Rather than call Jim, I told him that I would pay the debt at the end of the night. This was the only debt that I agreed to pay but paying this debt assured my safety from everyone else that was looking for Jim.

After a few days, I decided it was kind of crazy for me to stay in Harlem by myself. After all, I had gone all the way to New York to be with him. Therefore, I moved to downtown New York, and to a whole new set of problems. I moved to a hotel near Jim. Separate hotels were his idea, since Cathy had joined us in the city. He wanted to be able to run freely between both hotels. This worked well for me, because I liked my freedom. The freedom to go shopping, while he was still sleeping. Usually, as a result of staying out late at the clubs, he slept until early afternoon. On the other hand, I was willing to rise early to do my favorite thing, shop. Unless he made a special effort, which wasn't often, by the time he got up, I was gone. I was sending boxes of clothes home to Earline, regularly. Both hotels were full of people involved in some kind of hustle. If you tipped the person on the front desk right, you could get away with just about anything. In the one where I was living, you could only get on the elevator with permission. If trouble was following behind me into the hotel, I dropped money on the counter and ran for the elevator. Drugs weren't quite as abundant as they were in Harlem, but they were running a close race.

Although, we were staying in close proximity to each other, I seldom saw Cathy or Jim. Our escapades were taking us in different directions. Most of mine were taking me to overnight trips to jail. Where Cathy's trips took her remains a mystery until this day. One day she went to work and never returned. There were lots of rumors about her disappearance. Mostly the talk on the street was that she ran off with another pimp. Jim and I called every hospital in the area trying to locate someone that may have turned up as a Jane Doe, to no avail. All I know is that she went to work one night without taking any of her belongings and never returned. Several months later, he would claim that he had heard from her, but I knew that he was lying. The look of concern was still on his face. After Cathy's disappearance, I moved into the hotel with Jim, but kept my other room.

While we were in New York, Jim met a new set of friends and developed a new kind of habit. This was something that he tried to keep away from me, both the habit and the friends. I walked in on him and his friends one night and they had a pipe. He insisted that I leave. Later, I would learn this was free-basing cocaine. It became obvious that he was up to something again. Jim began easing some of his clothes to another room in the hotel. He told me that he was working on something, but gave me no details. One night, I returned early to the hotel room. The telephone was ringing. This was Jim, calling from the airport. He told me to grab what I could and meet him in Columbus, because he had just taken a large sum of money (tens of thousands) from someone on a drug deal. His new friends had given him the money to make a large drug transaction. He had gone in one door of the building and out another door. I was about $15 short of the airplane fare. There wasn't enough time for me to get the additional funds. My life was in danger if I was caught in the room. There wasn't enough time for me to clear my belongings from two hotels.

Leaving most of my belongings, I caught the next bus to Columbus. With each mile of the trip, I got angrier. Again, I had been innocently caught in one of his plots. When I got to Columbus, there was a major distance between us, and this wasn't a physical distance. He didn't care, because he was busy getting high. He was having fun smoking dope with his friends. A few weeks later, he moved back to Atlanta and I stayed in Columbus. He soon asked me to join him in Atlanta. Within a month, he had smoked up all the money. Deciding to go would be a huge mistake. Not because I was going to be with him, but because I was still upset with him, and this was going to leave me vulnerable to making another mistake. He was staying with one of his friends and didn't have anywhere for me to stay. This wasn't an appealing situation for me. After visiting with him for a very short period time, less than hour, I decided not to stay in Atlanta. I decided to go back to Columbus, but first, I needed to make a stop. This was a stop that would land me directly in front of hell's hatchway.

Charlotte Russell
Hope fading

Oh God This Is Hell

And there shall be weeping and gnashing of teeth.

While I was in Atlanta, I decided to pick up the clothes that I had left with my husband, several months earlier. I didn't know where he was staying, but I knew someone who would be able to help me. I stopped by Doug's apartment. To my surprise, this is where he was staying. Again, my false pride was going to cause me a lot of problems. Robert was involved with someone else. I wanted to prove that I could take him back. This would only bring more sorrow to my life. Again we would reconcile, and within a month, the beatings would start again. We moved into an apartment in East Point, Georgia. I began working at Arrow Shirt Factory, but financially I was dependent on Robert.

The harvest is past, the summer is ended, and we are not saved. Jeremiah 8:20

Shortly after my twenty-first birthday, my journey to hell accelerated. Robert continued his affairs, knowing that he had the upper hand in the relationship. Arrow was on short time, and we were often sent home early. One day when I returned home early from work, Robert has just returned from a previous night's fling. He was in the apartment with one of his friends and there was a woman present. There was nothing going on, therefore, I wasn't really concerned about them being there. However, he knew his guilt and began to beat me, immediately. That day, he moved in with the woman. I made another one of those foolish vows. Before I would allow a man to beat me again, I would kill him. After taking some newspaper and rolling it up tightly, the newspaper was placed under the head of my bed. I also placed a bottle of kerosene and a cigarette lighter beside the kerosene lamp located on the glass nightstand hanging next to the bed. The nightstand was suspended from the ceiling, next to the bed. This was a black macramé item that I had made, with a glass pane in the center.

During the next weeks, my financial status would reach a low that I had never experienced before. What would make the situation increasingly difficult was knowing that I had the ability to get the money that I needed within a few hours. In the luxury of the project, I had never seen a dispossessory notice, been close to eviction, or even experienced the lights or the telephone being turned off. Suddenly, I was faced with all of the above. To me, the thought of not being able to take care of my child was worse than any of my previous experiences. Self-pity became my friend and lulled me into deep dark depression. What was gnawing at my insides was knowing that the approximately $500 I needed was easy money. If I went down to Peachtree Street, I could probably talk my way up on this money before the day was over. This wasn't an option with Robert in the same city. Knowing that he would track me down if he couldn't find me, I was afraid to be caught on Peachtree. Although, he was living with someone else, I knew that he was still keeping track of everything that I was doing. Compounding my financial troubles would be my need to smoke marijuana to cope with my miserable life.

My mother had just given her life to Jesus. When I called to explain my situation, she encouraged me to surrender my life to Jesus, too. My mind was so consumed by my problems that I couldn't hear her witnessing to me. She gave me some suggestions of agencies that might be able to help me. When I called these agencies, there were no funds available. I called my landlord and explained the situation. She agreed that I could pay half the rent promptly and the rest later. The day I paid the agreed upon amount, half of the rent, I returned home to find a dispossessory notice on the door. Feeling there was nowhere to turn, I began to contemplate my options. Suicide seemed increasingly more appealing; at least if I were dead, my family would take care of my child.

There is a way, which seemeth right unto man, but the end thereof are the ways of death. Proverbs 14:12

In an act of desperation, I called Robert. He worked at the Omni and another hotel near Hartsfield Airport. The apartment was located in East Point, Georgia, part of metro Atlanta. This night he was working near the airport. He promised to bring me some money that night, as soon as he got off. He also asked me to run him some bath water, in about ten minutes. The airport was less than ten minutes away. I ran the water, but he never showed up. After an hour passed, it became apparent that he wasn't coming. Somehow, I had obtained the telephone number of the woman that he was staying with. In a panic, I dialed the number. When he answered the telephone, all I could do was hang up the telephone.

Well, there was one person who had always filled in the gaps when I needed something, Jim. What did I have to lose? Deciding to take my chances, I tracked him down. He was working at a bonding company in downtown Atlanta. With my daughter in tow, I went downtown to see him. This was another dead end. This time, he wouldn't be able to help me. Jim's new found drug habit was consuming all of his money. This wasn't what I expected. Jim always had money. At least for most of the years of our relationship, the amount of money that I needed would have only been a measly request. Now, I really needed to get high. All of my alternatives were running out. I had a friend who lived nearby. As usual, she had wine and marijuana. Sending my daughter to a back room, I began to get high. The thought of going home wasn't very appealing to me, and I didn't have to work the next day. I decided that it was better to spend the night at her apartment, avoiding driving home high. Early the next morning I returned home.

But I cried to him, My God, who lives forever, don't take my life while I am still so young! Psalm 102:24 NLT

On February 21, 1980, a life that had been spinning towards hell for years found its destination. Robert had arrived at the apartment before I got there and was getting ready for work. Deciding to go back to bed, I undressed and put on a peach chiffon negligee. My daughter went to her room to play. Robert called his supervisor at the hotel near the airport and informed him that he would be late. He stated that he had some business that he needed to finish. After hanging up the telephone, he began to beat me, kicking me, stomping me and pounding my head on the floor. This time the beating was more brutal than ever before. While he was pounding my head with his fist, several times I began to slip into unconsciousness. However, the next blow would bring me back around. This beating lasted well over an hour. Periodically, he would stop and continue getting ready for work, calling his supervisor each time, telling him that his business was taking longer than expected.

Fearing the beating was never going to stop, I told my daughter to go next door to the neighbor's apartment. From there, my daughter called the police, explaining what was going on at our apartment. When the police arrived, Robert heard them at the front door. Rather than opening the door, he spoke to them through the bedroom window. He explained that it was only a disagreement between him and his wife, and this was over now. Without ever seeing me, or asking to speak with me, they walked off, leaving me with a man that was trying to beat me to death. Immediately, he began kicking and striking me with his fists again. Remembering the newspaper under the bed and the kerosene, I decided to make my move when he took his next break.

While he was in the bathroom shaving, I removed the rolled newspaper from under the bed and doused it with kerosene from the bottle on the side of the bed. Making sure he didn't hear me approaching, I crept to the outside of the bathroom entrance. Trembling, I lit the newspaper and threw it into the bathroom without looking to see if it hit the target. Too afraid to watch my aim, I missed him and ran back to the bedroom. When he followed me into the room, I was sitting on the bed still holding the cigarette lighter. Angrily, he asked me if I had tried to kill him. Although terrified, I still responded that I had tried to kill him. Grabbing the bottle of kerosene from the nightstand, he moved towards the end of the bed, and snatched the cigarette lighter from my hand.

He said, "I'll pour this all over you."

While he was standing there with the bottled aimed to splash the kerosene on me, the picture froze in my mind. At this point that things began to move rapidly. With the cigarette lighter in his right hand and the bottle of kerosene in his left hand, he extended his arm and began to splash a small amount of kerosene on the negligee. With his arm extended I was able to reach for the bottle in his hand. With this action I also made a foolish declaration.

"You don't have to. I'll do it."

Taking the bottle from his hand, I splashed the kerosene oil all over my negligee. Afterwards, I handed him the bottle. He placed the bottle on the dresser located to the left of the bed, and turned to finish his task. The cigarette lighter was now in my right hand, and ready. There was no way that I was going to let him hit me again. My decision was made; I was ready to die to stop him. Anything was better than living like this, or so I thought. Holding the lighter in my hand, I flicked the lighter, hoping this would make him back off. A desperate assertion was made.

"If you come near me again, I'll light it."

Meaning that if he attempted to hit me again, I would light the negligee. My assumption was that death would be immediate relief. By this time, he had been beating me so long that he had completely lost control. When he drew back to hit me again, I jumped, accidentally igniting the negligee. What was only seconds would seem like an eternity.

The negligee was made out of layers of chiffon. It was only the negligee that was burning, but it seemed like the whole room was full of flames, and I was in the middle of an unquenchable fire. This was a glimpse of hell. Immediately rolling across the bed, I attempted to quench the flames, but this failed to extinguish the flames. Remembering the stop, drop, and roll, I dropped to the floor. Robert tried to assist me with rolling across the carpet on the floor. The flame refused to be quenched, and this process didn't work either. I stood up and began to pull the negligee over my head.

When the remnants of the gown were nearing my eyes, an authoritative voice spoke from heaven.

"Pull it back down."

I obeyed without a second thought. It was then that I remembered the water that was still in the bathtub from the night before. Running with lightening speed, I ran to the bathroom and jumped into the tub. This was too late; the damage had been done. While I was looking down, the skin that I loved so much turned black and drew up like a raisin. Robert's fury was burning, hotter than my skin. The site of my charred skin made him angrier and he raised his fist to hit me again. For no reason that made any sense, I assured him that I would be fine.

"It's okay."

He lowered his fist and began cursing. Somehow I understood that he was furious, scared, and sorry all at the same time. Yet he was so trapped by his anger that the only way he found release was in physically abusing women.

Sudden coldness began to chill me to my bones. The fire was gone but my skin was still burning. At the same time, I was so cold. When I got out of the tub, I went in my daughter's room not wanting to return to the burning room. Things seemed to go extremely fast from here. Trembling and freezing, I was struggling to stay calm. I wanted to wrap myself in the comforter on the bed, but I was afraid for anything to touch me. Robert was pacing back and forth, still angry. There was no anger or malice left in me.

At this point things happened so fast that I'm not certain what happened. When the paramedics got there they were asking a lot of questions and telling me not to go into shock. My mind was on more important things. I was dying and I knew that I had a first class ticket to hell. The glimpse that I had of hell was enough to convince me that I didn't want to go there.

Praying I said, "God let me pass out, but please don't let me die. Give me a chance to find out what it takes not to go to hell."

In the back of the ambulance they were working frantically, telling me to remain calm, and to hang on. Amidst the sound of the siren, I continued to pray.

"Let me pass out, but don't let me die. I don't want to go to hell."

Unto thee will I cry, O Lord my rock; be not silent to me: lest, if thou be silent to that go down to the pit. Psalm 28:1

The pain was unlike anything that I had ever imagined or that I can describe presently. Willing myself to slip into unconsciousness wasn't working; yet, I knew that I could die if I wanted to. For over a month I had thought that I coveted death because the frustrations of my situation were unbearable. At the moment that I had the opportunity, I realized that I was far from being prepared to die. The thought of enduring for an eternity, what I had endured in the burning bedroom for seconds, wasn't appealing. The desires for death vanished. In the place of my foolish thoughts was a longing to find out how I could avoid spending an eternity in hell.

"Please God, don't let me die!"

Therefore my heart is glad, and my glory rejoiceth: my flesh also shall rest in hope. For thou will not leave my soul in hell.
Psalm 6:9-10

ANGELS UNAWARE

I will lift up my eyes unto the hills from which cometh my help.

In the emergency room, the medical staff continued to ask endless questions. All I wanted to do was pass out. If I understood anything, it was that things would get worse if my uncles knew what had happened that day. Robert had already killed one person, and I knew that he was capable of doing this again. Years later, he would kill his best friend of more than twenty years, during a domestic altercation, and never shed a tear. I didn't want anybody else to get hurt. Desperately, I wanted to block everything that had happened out of my mind. After all, everything else ceased to be important. The things that they were asking about seemed trivial. As they continued to ask their questions, silently in my mind I continued.

"Please God let me pass out, but don't let me die."

Audibly I continued with one request, "Please give me something for the pain!"

The answers continuously came back, "First we have to gather some information."

There were no thoughts of revenge in my mind. There was one thing that was important. I needed to find out how to avoid going to hell. Finally, I lost track of what was going on. They must have given me something for the pain.

I love the Lord, because he hath heard my voice and my supplications. Because he hath inclined his ear unto me, therefore will I call upon him as long as I live. The sorrows of death compassed me, and the pains of hell gat hold upon me: I found trouble and sorrow. Then called I upon the name of the Lord; O Lord, I beseech thee, deliver my soul. The Lord preserveth the simple: I was brought low, and he helped me. Return unto thy rest, O my soul; for the Lord hath dealt bountifully with thee. For thou hast delivered my soul from death, mine eyes from tears, and my feet from falling. Psalm 116:1-8

Later, I would wake up in the Intensive Care Unit of the Burn Unit at Grady Hospital drowsy and in severe pain. I was told that second and third degree burns covered 70% of my body, but I had no idea what a second or third degree burn was. My wildest imagination couldn't envision what this meant. I understood that I was still alive, and that was about the depth of my understanding. I had no idea how serious my condition was or that my life was still in jeopardy. My request to pass out had been granted, but I hadn't died. Therefore, I assumed I wasn't dying.

The burns began directly below my eyes and extended to directly above my knees, both my front and back torso had been burned. My chest area was completely flat, and with the exception of the name on the chart at the foot of my bed, there was no indication that the body in the bed belonged to a woman. Both of my arms and my legs were wrapped in bulky wraps, with only my hands and feet exposed. From below my eyes to the top of my thighs, I was covered with a white cream. There was something that looked like a diaper folded over my pubic area. In what could only be described as a miracle within itself, this area had remained unscathed by the fire. This would be my only clothing for most of the time that I would be in the hospital. My body was totally exposed for everyone entering the room to see.

Although I couldn't see myself clearly, I was worried about how it would affect my mother to see me in this condition. They had told me she was on her way to the hospital. Mama entered the room with my Aunt Bobbie, while I was wondering about this. Immediately, I began to apologize to her for putting her through this crisis. She assured me that she was glad that God had spared her to be there for me.

Consistently she repeated, "I thank God that He allowed me the chance to be here for you."

My aunt had tried to prepare my mother for what she would see when she entered my room. My mother later said that I looked like a raw catfish, when she walked in the room. However, on her face that day she showed no signs of disgust at the sight before her. Aunt Bobbie told me recently that when they went to the apartment, my flesh was still in the bathtub.

My aunt is a real comedian and she wanted me to laugh. She told me that when she was told about what had happened to me she ran to the car. There was only one problem. She was running so fast that she missed the car. She slid up under the car and had to be pulled from under the car. Bobbie had been drinking, but she was sober now. This would begin a continuous routine of them visiting me. These two people would be the only ones to weather the storm out. Mama spent five days in Atlanta, on her first visit, before returning to Columbus, and returned every weekend to visit me during the remainder of my stay in the hospital. When she went back to Columbus the first time she took Earline back with her, to live with Ma'Dear. Aunt Bobbie came several times a day, for almost three months, until the nurses asked her to skip a day. They said that I was getting too dependent on her.

Two detectives came to the hospital. They had been questioning Robert about what had happened. They wanted me to make a statement to enable them to press charges against him. My mind was made up; it was best for everyone if no one knew what had happened inside the apartment. The morphine had made my mind cloudy; I don't remember what I said. They were standing near the foot of my bed. I wasn't willing to assist them with the investigation. It was too painful to repeat what had happened in the house. There would be a long time before I would be able to tell my mother what had occurred on this day, months after I was released from the hospital. Aunt Bobbie said I told her one-day while I was in the hospital, but I don't remember telling either of them. At some point I began assuming that I had told Mama what happened.

Perhaps as a result of the extensive painkillers that I was taking or an unconscious effort to block out pain that was too horrible to imagine, my memory of most things that happened that year remains sketchy. After I threw the newspaper in the bathroom, for years there were only flashes of memory. The picture of Robert at the foot of the bed with the bottle of kerosene aimed to pour remained clear and frozen in my mind. My sitting on the bed frightened, and cowering with nowhere to run remained. Robert getting ready to hit me again was never forgotten. Rolling across the bed while the gown was burning was unforgettable. I don't remember what the bedroom looked like other than the head of the bed being near the window, and the night stand that I had made hanging from the ceiling. Rolling across the floor is clear. The room burning and the voice speaking to me are the clearest memory. Sitting in the tub watching my skin change, with Robert ready to continue beating me is clear. Sitting on Earline's bed, almost going into shock is clear. The paramedics arriving is hazy. Being in the back of the ambulance, praying was always clear, but not the ride to the hospital. The next clear memory is being examined in the emergency room, and then my memory jumps to a hazy memory of two faceless detectives standing at the foot of my bed.

Later that first day, a nurse came in to change my bed. Her name was Ms. Davis but there are other names that better suit her personality, that are currently inappropriate for me to use. Mama and Bobbie were in the waiting room. This was the second time that my hospital bed had been changed, since I arrived in Intensive Care. She instructed me to move to one side of the bed to enable her to change the sheets. Explaining that I didn't have the strength to move, I asked her to place my legs in the stirrups hanging over the bed. This would allow me to press down on the lower portion of my legs, which would lift my bottom from the sheets. The lower portion of my legs weren't burnt. This was the way the last nurse had changed the sheets.

Ms. Davis explained, "I've been a nurse for fifteen years and you don't tell me what you can and can't do."

She further explained, "If you don't move, I'll snatch the sheets from under you."

To this I responded, "I don't know how I'm going to do it, but if you snatch these sheets, somehow, I am going to get the strength to knock the "H" out of you."

Ms. Davis told me, "This is exactly why you are in this predicament, and you need to be praying."

She didn't change the sheets. My skin was sensitive, and during the next months the sheets would require frequent changing. Even lint on the bed irritated my raw skin. Scratch that, this wasn't my skin that was irritated; this was my flesh.

This wasn't the only uncompassionate nurse who had chosen the wrong profession that I would encounter. This would only be the first one. This was a warning of things to come. Over the next months, nurses would often come into the room and without even taking time to introduce themselves, they would begin to question me. Rather than asking how I was feeling or if I needed anything, they would ask the same horrible question.

"What happened to you?"

Pretending to ignore these questions became an art. This was my secret and I was keeping it. After awhile, I became an expert at discerning their motives and intentions in asking this question. When curiosity rather than compassion was driving the question, I closed my eyes and prayed that the nurse would never be assigned to care for me again.

When my mother and aunt returned to the room, I told them what Ms. Davis had said to me. They went back to the nurses' station and my aunt informed the head nurse of what had taken place. Mama and Bobbie went to the family waiting room and cried. This was one of those bad things that worked out for my good. It was thus that I met Agatha Story. She was my angel that would see me through this difficult time. Apologizing for Ms. Davis, she assured my mother that she would take care of me whenever she was on duty. Ms. Davis would rarely be allowed to take care of me. On the days that Ms. Davis was my nurse, she wrote the same note in my medical chart.

"Complained, Complained."

After four days in Intensive Care, I was moved into a room. I was placed on a curricular bed. This bed would serve to turn me from my back to my stomach. If I wasn't secured properly for the turn, my body would slip slightly, causing me extreme pain. This process was extremely scary. It required two people to flip me on the bed, one standing on each side of the bed. I would close my eyes and pray that the flip would be over quickly. These beds also had the ability to position me in an upright position, temporarily, allowing more opportunity for my body to slip.

I learned quickly to request a shot (pain medication) thirty minutes prior to being moved. Even the slightest movement of my body caused severe pain. The medication didn't stop the pain, but helped to make it endurable. They would move me from my bed by lifting my body with the sheets on my bed. Each corner of the sheet was gripped to enable the sheet to serve as a lift, moving me from the bed onto the stretcher. There was no way to move me without pain, but if they managed to move me quickly and in unison, this was more tolerable.

Continue to love each other with true Christian love. Don't forget to show hospitality to strangers, for some who have done this have entertained angels without realizing it! Don't forget about those in prison. Suffer with them as though you were there yourself. Share the sorrow of those being mistreated, as though you feel the pain in your own bodies. Hebrew 13:13 NLT

Story was true to her word and would go beyond her duties as a nurse. She would read the Bible to me often during her shift. Story's favorite Psalm was the 121. She never forgot to read this one in addition to the other scriptures. After the first time she read this, it became my favorite Psalm. Knowing that I was overly concerned about my feet, the only part of my body that was still pretty, she would give me a pedicure whenever the polish was removed from my toes before surgery. Every other day there was some kind of surgical procedure performed. Therefore, Story had lots of opportunities to care for my feet.

Whenever, I woke up to discover my toes weren't painted, I became agitated. Nobody wanted to rub ugly feet, and I wanted everybody entering my room to rub my feet. My feet were itching constantly, and I couldn't scratch them. Everybody that came to visit me had to rub my feet, not that there were a lot of visitors. Whenever anybody asked what he or she could do for me, to their surprise, I responded, "Would you please just rub my feet?" The traditional things that you bring to a hospital room weren't applicable to me. There was no need for nightgowns, flowers, robes, slippers, under garments, or even fruit. I wouldn't be wearing anything anytime soon, and I wouldn't be getting up from the bed to walk around.

I was totally dependent on others to feed me, change me, bath me, brush my teeth, and comb my hair. Without the protection of my skin, my level of comfort was constantly changing from one extreme to another. First, I would be hot and they would feed me ice to cool me down. The ice made me cold, so they turned the heat lamp on me, and gave me a cup of coffee. Afterwards, I was hot and the cycle repeated itself. There was no way to cover my body. Unable to sit up, I had to eat and drink everything lying flat on my back. Mama prayed for me to be able to swallow medication from this position.

Unable to ring a buzzer to call the nurse when I needed assistance, if I needed anything, I had to scream until someone heard me. While in the hospital, I didn't drink water. Water was something that I had never acquired a taste for. Usually, I alternated between Kool-Aid and coffee. I didn't like coffee; this was a necessity to help me deal with the chills. To eliminate the problem of having to continuously give me something cold to drink, to cool my body, someone came up with a unique idea. Since the flow of liquids into my mouth was almost a constant drip between hot and cold, this made someone think about an IV for my mouth. The pitcher on my bed table remained full of Kool-Aid. An IV tube was hooked inside the pitcher, draped over my bed, and positioned with tape near my mouth. This enabled me to barely tilt my head to sip the Kool-Aid. This worked well since it kept me from screaming as regular, and helped to limit the number of times the nurses had to run in and out of my room.

To make matters worse, someone had to feed me without dropping anything on my exposed flesh. If there is anything worse than being hungry and not having anything to eat, it's having the food sitting in front of you but being unable to feed yourself. Often, the nurses forgot to come back to feed me until after the food was cold. It was hard to eat laying flat on my back. But it was almost impossible to eat cold food from this position. My weight was dropping, and they were giving me Ensure to drink as a dietary supplement.

Unable to even ring the buzzer to request the assistance of a nurse, my cries for help were sometimes interpreted as complaining. To avoid this, my aunt would begin to provide most of my routine care. Arriving at the hospital before breakfast, she would assure that I was fed with care and in a timely manner. She would leave from the hospital allowing just enough time to arrive at her job at the appointed time. In the evenings, she would return from work to feed me my dinner. Scraping the Silvadine ointment from the wounds also required a lot of patience to avoid hurting me. After several bad experiences with this, I was afraid for most of the nurses to touch me. Some of the nurses seemed impatient to get the cream changed. Their hastiness caused me immense pain. My Aunt Bobbie would request permission to perform this task, too. There was no way to alleviate all the pain associated with this procedure, but at least she would make every effort not to unnecessarily hurt me.

The visitors soon dwindled down after it became apparent that I wasn't going to die and this was going to be a long healing process. However, I don't think anybody imagined how long the recovery would be. The detectives didn't come back either, since it was apparent that I wasn't going to explain what happened in the house. Several nurses would become extremely special to my family during this time. This provided my mother with much needed assurance when she returned to Columbus each Sunday night. They would take care of me until she returned the following Friday afternoon.

My recovery was also going to strain my mother's finances, but she was determined that she would come to see me every weekend. She was also determined to keep the television in my room turned on. Grady charged a small daily fee to rent the television. One day my television was turned off. When my roommate's husband came to see her, he asked about her television.

"Can I get your T.V. turned on?"

Pointing to me, she said, "No, get hers turned on."

This would be one of the many people that God would touch to show kindness to me, while most of my family closed their eyes to the trauma that I was experiencing.

My road to recovery was going to be much longer than I imagined. Doctors and psychiatrists attempted to prepare Mama and me for the long road ahead. However, we had no point of reference to relate to this process. We had never experienced anything of this magnitude or even imagined anyone being burned this severely. The only thing that I equated the process of a burn healing was the healing process that occurs when you're burned by a steam iron. This picture wasn't preparing me for the intensity of my recovery.

In the day when I cried thou answereth me, and strengthenedst me with strength in my soul. Psalm 138:3

There were other angels in the burn unit at Grady, Addie and Linda Tolliver. I can't remember Addie's last name, but I have never forgotten how very special she treated me at a time when I needed someone to care about me. They were both more than nurses. They had a special gift to work in this unit that reeked with the smell of burned flesh, and was often engulfed with clamors that ranged from moans to screams. There were no signs of frustration or impatience from them when I constantly requested their services to do for me what I couldn't do for myself. Rather than becoming upset with me, they continuously made every effort to make me comfortable. Nothing made me comfortable, but they never stopped trying.

CAN YOU REALLY SAVE ANYBODY

My help cometh from the Lord who made heaven and earth…

There was a great deal of concern at this time about my mental well-being. Hospital social workers and psychiatrists would visit me regularly to see how I was coping emotionally with the trauma. Apparently, the constant pain, and the change in my physical appearance were enough to cause me to have a nervous breakdown. They didn't understand how thankful I was to be alive. My soul had become more important than my physical appearance. Somehow, I think they thought this was a crutch. The social worker would make arrangements for me to have a stereo in my room to listen to gospel music. She came to see me often.

During this time, an overwhelming sense of gratitude had engulfed me. On this floor at Grady there were patients that had been burned over various parts of their body. There were patients that had experienced burns anywhere that you can imagine, including the places that I hadn't been burned. My first roommate was an elderly lady. While intoxicated, she had sat in a tub of hot water. She died from these burns. Some burns by nature of their location caused them to be more life threatening, and patients at Grady were dying from these kinds of burns. I had been spared all of these places. There were babies that had been burned. The only way to communicate their pain was with constant cries. There was constant pain on this ward.

The right hand of the Lord is exalted: the right hand of the Lord doeth valiantly. I shall but live, to declare the works of the Lord. The Lord hath chastened me sore: but he hath not given me over to death. Psalm 118:16-18

It quickly became apparent to me that in the midst of this tragedy, I had been tremendously blessed. It was remarkably obvious that the hand of God had been upon me during the fire. All of my vital organs had been spared. My lips had been burned but not the inside of my mouth. My nose had been burned but not the inside of my nostrils. My ears were burned but not the inside of my ears. Beneath my eyes had been burned but not my eyes. There were several knots on my head from the brutality of the beating. In addition, my hair had been scorched but not my scalp. By what can only be characterized as a miracle, my other vital organs were also spared. God had been with me in the fiery furnace just as He had with Sha'-drach, Me'-shach, and A-bed'-ne-go.

One day while I was looking at television, I heard that Richard Pryor had been seriously burned while freebasing cocaine. I followed his recovery closely, sympathetic to his pain. It wasn't long before he was released from the hospital. He began making jokes about what had happened to him. The way he joked about being burned hurt me and I resented this. This may have been his way of coping with his own internal pain, but for me there was nothing amusing or entertaining about the pain or the blazing flames that were still raging inside my body.

Out of the depths have I cried unto thee, O Lord. Lord, hear my voice: let thine ears be attentive to the voice of my supplications. If thou shouldest mark iniquities, O Lord, who will stand? But there is forgiveness with thee, that thou mayest be feared. I wait for the Lord, my soul doth wait, and in his word do I hope. Psalm 130:1-5

Story continued to read the 121 Psalm to me each time that she was on duty. This was our favorite scripture. She was very patient and attentive to my needs. Love flowed from her in actions and deeds. There are no words that will ever be able to express my gratitude to her, since she is a living testament of the love of my Lord and Savior Jesus Christ. Story kept my feet pedicured. She purchased the tools for this task. She understood how concerned I was about my feet. I shared with Story the things that I couldn't tell anybody else. She witnessed to me with her actions, and I looked forward to the days that she would be working.

And suddenly there shined round about him a light from heaven. Acts 9:3

The hand of the Lord was upon me, and carried me out in the spirit of the Lord, and set me down in the midst of the valley which was full of bones, and caused me to pass by them round about: and, behold, there were very many in the open valley; and, lo, they were very dry. And he said unto me, Son of man, can these bones live? And I answered, O Lord God, thou knoweth. Again he said unto me, Prophesy upon these bones, and say unto them, O ye dry bones, hear the word of the Lord. Thus saith the Lord God unto these bones; Behold, I will cause breath to enter into you, and ye shall live: And I will lay sinews upon you and bring flesh upon you, and cover you with skin, and put breath in you, and ye shall live; and ye shall know that I am the Lord. Ezekiel 37:1-6

One night, someone patting my hand awakened me from my sleep. Assuming this was Story, I was surprised but not afraid to see only a brilliant light. There was an incredible sense of peace in my room. This light enabled me to see my body for the first time in its entirety. Until this time, most of my movements had been confined to being flipped on my circular bed or being transferred from my bed to a stretcher. Whenever I would leave the room I was headed to the patient elevator. Having lived in Columbus most of my life, I wasn't familiar with the hospital. This night, I would leave the room heading to a different elevator, the public elevator. This magnificent calming light took me from the room to the passenger elevator. We boarded this elevator and went down to the main entrance of Grady. The light guided me down a flight of stairs and out the front of the hospital. We took a journey from Atlanta to Columbus via the expressway. On the way to Columbus, I saw my life prior to my entering the hospital. All of my sins were candidly revealed to me. There were scenes from Peachtree, scenes from Columbus, and scenes from New York City. Clearly manifested to me was the wickedness of my lifestyle. There was no doubt that this lifestyle led directly to hell.

Once we arrived in Columbus at Warren Williams Apartments the nature of the scenes changed. Along with my mother and my daughter, I was headed to church. I was walking to the car with them. The light took me back up the expressway and along the way I saw what my life would be like in the future. I was going to recover. We returned to Grady, entering through a back door of the hospital. Once we entered the elevator, a finger reached over and pushed the button for the tenth floor. The light returned me to the room and gently placed me back in the bed. Through all of this I wasn't afraid.

For I neither received it of man, neither was I taught it, but by the revelation of Jesus Christ. Galatians1:12

It was obvious that Jesus wanted to save me. Me! In all of my filthiness, all of my wretchedness, He wanted to save Me! He had died for me—damaged goods. There was nothing lovable about me. I didn't even love me. There was nothing morally good about me. Yet for this Charlotte, He had died. Not for a Charlotte that was nice and clean, but one who was a Black Sheep. He had laid down His life willingly. Me! He died for me. In all of my wretchedness, He died for me. He had forgiven me for every single thing that I had ever done.

Afterwards, I wanted to share this with Story, but I was afraid she would think that I was loosing my mind or hallucinating. Screaming to the top of my voice, I called for Story. When she arrived, rather than telling her what had happened, I began to question her about the hospital. After she confirmed that my description of the hospital was accurate, she wanted to know why I was asking all the questions. It was only then that I explained what had happened.

"Story, I just saw the Lord."

This was recorded in my hospital records. Thus it was then that I realized God really loved even a horrible sinner like me. In all my wretchedness, His grace was sufficient enough to save me. This precious grace gave me the ability to cope with the years ahead. My recovery wasn't going to take weeks or months; this was going to take years. This wasn't apparent to me at the time. Not only was I unable to feed myself, which I thought I would be able to do whenever the bandages were removed, I was unable to walk, and to perform even basic functions for myself. The doctors had warned me not to sleep with a pillow under my head. Uncomfortable without the pillow and not understanding the reasoning for not using the pillow, I continued to request the pillow to support my head. This would cause my neck to heal in a constricted position. The burns had affected my body in ways that I didn't even begin to understand.

When asking can God really save anybody? I'm not asking because of a liar named Peter or a Christian persecutor named Paul. It's not the woman of Samaria at the well or the woman caught in adultery that I'm worried about. It's not a tax collector name Zacchaeus that doesn't measure up. It's not Mary Magdalene, whose sins are innumerable. It's not Rahab the harlot that's damaged goods. It's not for the Pharisees or the Sadducees. It's not because of the Roman solders that nailed Him to the cross. It's not the drunk or the junkie on the street that seems hopeless. It's not the serial killer or serial rapist who has committed heinous crimes. It's not the child molester who has distorted children's lives. When I ask this question, I want to know about me. I'm the one that seems hopeless.

"God, I'm damaged. I'm used. I'm broken. I'm marred. I'm scared. Oh God, you know that I have done some horrible things. God you have seen all the things that I have done. God I failed so many times."

"God, can you save a nobody like me?"

"In spite of all I have done, can you save me?'

"God, can you save a somebody as horrible as I am?"

Without a doubt, the answer is, "For God sent not His son into the world to condemn the world; but that the world through Him might be saved."

God doesn't condemn us of our sin. He convicts us of our sins that we might go and sin no more. Condemnation leaves us ashamed and without hope, whereas, conviction alerts us to our sins, while pointing us to the saving grace of the Savior. Grace is Gods unmerited favor. While grace is freely provided to us, it cost God everything, His only begotten Son. God loves the sinner, but hates the sin. He loves us in spite of ourselves. He's been good in spite of me. There is nothing that we can do to earn His love or acceptance. When we accept Christ as our Savior, God no longer sees our wretchedness; He sees only the blood that Jesus shed for the remission of our sins. He looks at us and sees what we have the potential to become. He refines us and molds us into vessels of honor.

> *Wherefore I was made a minister, according to the gift of the grace of God unto me by the effectual working of his power. Unto me, who was less than the least of all saints, is this grace given, that I should preach among the Gentiles the unsearchable riches of Christ.* Ephesians 3:7-8

That I may know Him, and the power of His resurrection, and the fellowship of His sufferings, being made comformable unto His death.

Philippians 3:10

THE RECOVERY ROAD

*And a highway shall be there, and a way, and it shall be called
The way of Holiness*

My first stay at Grady would be three months and five days. Not that I remember this, since I was heavily medicated most of the time that I was in the hospital. The medication affected portions of my memory, or perhaps I deliberately chose to block out some of the pain. My mother has filled in the gaps for most of what happened that year. Actually, it seems that I lost a year of my life, the year that so many look forward to, the twenty-first year. During the first months at Grady, there would be surgical procedures every other day. There would need to be continuous IVs. This was made increasingly more difficult by the percentages of my body covered with burns. My veins were already fine, and they began to collapse. In their efforts to locate a good vein, this often required two people working on each of my feet and each of my hands. A total of eight people were rubbing and popping, trying to get the veins to pop up.

> *Look here, you people that say, "Today or tomorrow we are going to a certain town and will stay there a year. We will do business there and make a profit." How do you know what will happen on tomorrow? For your life is like the morning fog—it's here a little while, then it's gone. What you ought to say is, "If the Lord wants us to, we will live and do this or that."* James 4:13-15

Although I had been burned when the weather was still cold, the day before, I took my Cocoa Butter bath and rubbed my legs down with Cocoa Butter Lotion, checking to be sure that my legs were without blemish. I was making plans to wear hot pants during the summer, and I wanted to be sure my legs were ready, taking for granted that when summer came, I would want to show my legs. Actually, indoors I never stopped wearing the hot pants. When I woke up in Intensive Care, I assumed I was going to live. I had no idea how serious my condition was. When I looked at the bandages on my legs and arms, I assumed that whenever they were removed I would be able to do all the things that I had done before I was burned.

There were so many things that I had taken for granted, like being able to brush my teeth whenever I woke up during the night. I hated the taste that would be in my mouth when I awakened during the night. At this time with all the medication that I was taking the taste was worse, but I could no longer brush my teeth. I dreamed of being able to do this again. Scratching my head when it itched was something that I had never given much thought. When my head itched, I attempted to no avail to explain to someone else where my head itched or hurt. Without the ability to even point to my head the task was almost impossible. Being able to turn or cover up in bed seemed only a natural thing to do. For weeks I remained basically in one position in the bed, weak and to scared to move for fear of the pain. The only times my body moved was when somebody else moved me. When I was told that I would be moving to a floor for physical therapy, I didn't want to leave my surrogate family on the burn unit. I had become comfortable there. The patients on this floor were like me. Besides that, why did I need physical therapy? All that I needed was for them to remove the bandages, or so I thought.

When the bandages came off, the physical therapist began coming to my room. Even my body being moved to a sitting position was a major task. I felt intoxicated, even though the process moved very slowly. The therapist waited for my meal to be served. I was ready to feed myself. She placed a special spoon in my hand, and when I attempted to bring a spoonful of food to my mouth, my hand, instead went over my head. I had absolutely no control over my arms or legs. During the last weeks at Grady, I would be moved to another floor for more extensive physical and occupational therapy. Here I would be taught how to feed and dress myself again. They would teach me how to stand up between rails. There would be endless exercises to stretch my neck and arms. Braces were made for my neck in an effort to help me hold my head up. There would be other exercises to strengthen my legs. Eventually, I would be taught to use a walker.

Learning to use the walker would allow me to leave the hospital on a weekend pass to my aunt's house. This wouldn't be just a challenge physically, but also emotionally. I was terrified that I would fall. The thought of how people would look at me once I went out into the public troubled me. As I walked towards the house, there were consistent stares from the people that were outside of the apartment. The sun was also a problem, since each time it would touch my skin I would burn all over again. The weekend trip ended without any major complications. Plans were being made for me to make the transition back to Columbus. There were several complications to this transition. At the time that I was burned, I had no insurance. Extensive physical and occupational therapy would be required if I was going to recover to a functional level. Additionally, I had no money or even appropriate clothes. The major and most pressing problem was however, that I didn't have a way to get home to Columbus.

My mother had a car but had never driven on the expressway in Columbus, and was afraid of the Atlanta traffic. She had probably never even driven a car over 30 mph.

My condition prevented me from being able to live alone. All of my belongings had now been in storage for several months. The things that had troubled and depressed me before the fire were now insignificant. Before being evicted, Mama had placed all my belongings in storage. These troubles didn't seem important anymore. Before I had worried about not being able to take care of my daughter, now I couldn't take care of either of us. It was necessary for me to return to my mother's house, the place that I left at sixteen. My return was totally different than the way I left. I left to be independent before reaching the age of maturity. Now at the age of maturity, I was returning, totally dependent.

During my weeks in the physical therapy ward, I met a male nurse named Frank. This was another angel that God put in my path. He would be extremely kind to me. For some reason that I can't imagine, he was attracted to me. I enjoyed the companionship, but I was far from being ready for a relationship. During this period I was now able to wear some loose clothing. He would keep my clothes washed for me. Additionally, he would take me out on the deck for picnics, when I was able to tolerate the weather. One day, he would ask me if I had a way to get home. He offered to drive me back to Columbus.

In preparation for my return home there were other things that needed to be addressed. I had no income, and would be unable to work for an extended period of time. The hospital social worker made arrangements for a representative from the Social Security Office to come to the hospital to meet with me. My doctors completed the paperwork for me to apply for disability. This was going to be a longer and more difficult process than I could have imagined.

There would be additional trips back to Grady for plastic surgery after my release from the hospital. Frank would volunteer to bring me home from these trips, too. The other problem would be getting to the hospital from Columbus. The Greyhound bus would be the only option, because only a limited number of people in my family were concerned about my recovery. None of these had a car. The ones who had cars weren't coming by to see me. Riding the bus would be extremely difficult and painful. Boarding the bus would require that I place one foot on the step of the bus, and grab the bars on both sides of the steps, inside the door, while my mother pushed me up from behind. The pain from this process lasted for most of the trip to Atlanta.

> *Don't turn away from me in my time of distress. Bend down your ear and answer me quickly when I call to you, for my days disappear like smoke, and my bones burn like red-hot coals. My heart is sick, withered like grass, and I have lost my appetite. Because of my groaning, I am reduced to skin and bones. I am like an owl in the desert, like a lonely owl in a far-off wilderness. I lie awake, lonely as a solitary bird on the roof. My enemies taunt me day after day. They mock me and curse me. I eat ashes instead of my food. My tears run down into my drink... Psalm 102:2-9 NLT*

Although, my muscles were still weak, I had moved from the walker to crutches. However, my body was almost bent in half, making it extremely difficult for me to look up. My weight was down to 98 pounds. The legs that I loved to show were almost instantly only sticks. Mama promised me that my legs would return. Each morning she prepared me cheese omelets, loaded with cheese. Almost every Saturday evening Mama prepared Sunday dinners. She usually cooked barbecue ribs, macaroni and cheese, collard greens, candied yams, corn bread, homemade ice cream, and pound cake.

Once I was home from the hospital, I would immediately fulfill my desire to attend church. This would be a major chore for everybody in the house. Let me say that I never quite mastered the crutches. Going up and down the two steps to get into our home was always a challenge. Additionally, going outside during daylight hours required extra precaution. With a large straw hat on my head and wrapped in a white sheet to protect my skin from the sun, I would need pillows to sit on and a hand fan in case I got hot. Each Sunday, we would start out with my gear. Sunday School would come off without a hitch, since attendance was sparse. Morning Worship was nearly impossible. As soon the crowd filled the church, about twenty minutes into the service, my mother would have to rush me from the church. My skin would be burning again. Once we reached the house, they would stack pillows on my bed, directly in front of the window air conditioning unit. While I sat on these pillows, my mother, sister and daughter would fan me until my body cooled again. Each Sunday, we would go through this routine again, while my tolerance increased. Eventually, I would be able to stay for the complete service.

My neck was almost completely constricted to my chest because the skin had meshed together during the healing process. In order for me to look up, it required that I strain, and almost tilt my body backwards. The same problem existed with both of my arms and my side. I was barely able to lift them from my sides. The first time I returned to Grady, 2 1/5 inches of skin was grafted from my body and placed between my chin and my chest, in an attempt to make me a neck. This is the only way that I can describe it, because it literally looked as though I didn't have a neck, the skin from my chin had so completely meshed with my chest. This procedure provided some release for my neck but not to the extent that the doctors had hoped. They wanted to perform an additional operation to correct the problem, but I opted against this second operation on this area.

After the donor sites healed, I returned to Grady for a second set of skin grafts. Originally they were only suppose to operate on one of my arms. When I arrived at the hospital the doctors informed me that they were going to do both arms, and a place on my side that was constricted. However, when they began the operation, they decided this would be too much for me to endure in one procedure.

My roommate during this procedure was having implants done. She told me that this was the third time that she had this procedure performed. This was the procedure that I was scheduled to have on my next trip. My conversation with her changed my mind. The thought of continuous surgeries wasn't appealing to me. God later performed this operation for me, and when He corrected this, He made the area better than it was before the damage caused by the fire. There would be no need for repeated surgeries to correct the problem.

The doctors at Grady had given me the name of a doctor to contact at the Medical Center in Columbus, once I returned home. When my situation was explained to him, he made financial arrangements for the cost of my therapy at the hospital to be waived. The cost of my care at Grady was also waived. Both occupational and physical therapy would be necessary several times a week for an extended period of time to facilitate my recovery. Shortly after approving my treatment, the doctor committed suicide.

Although, I had lots of family in Columbus, the burden of my care rested totally on my Mama. Ma'Dear tried to help financially and by taking care of my daughter. She bought my Job suit, an elastic suit designed to fit my body perfectly, while providing pressure to help the burns heal flat. This suit covered everything except my face, hands, and feet. My face had healed with no signs of the burns. The bottom of my legs hadn't been burned. For weeks, I had begged the doctors not to use them to remove skin for the skin grafts. After running out of other donor sites, they removed skin from the bottom of one of my legs for the grafts. This was extremely disappointing to me, because I had hoped to still be able to show the bottom of my legs.

It would be necessary for my mother to drop me off at the Medical Center Hospital several times a week before she went to work at 8:00 a.m. I make mention of this because a lot of things would need to occur before she dropped me off each morning. Unable to perform most basic functions for myself, these burdens fell to my mother. She was determined that I would regain my weight, which had been dropping since my hospitalization. Each morning she would cook my breakfast, iron my clothes, help me get dressed, and comb my wig. Oh yeah, I forgot to mention that my hair had been severely damaged by the fire and the anesthesia, and had been cut completely off before I left the hospital.

Getting me in and out of the bathtub was a major task. Mama had to carefully and meticulously ease me down into the tub. I didn't have enough muscle control to ease down in the tub or to stand up to get out of the tub myself or to even assist her. She would also have to lift me out of the tub. She did all of this by herself and she was always scared that I would fall, or that she would hurt my delicate skin and fragile body. It would become a challenge for me to one day surprise her by getting out of the tub unassisted. One day I was sure that I could get out unassisted. I had been practicing for weeks. Finally, I had enough nerve to try this. As I turned to grasp the side of the tub, I prayed that I wouldn't slip. Almost crawling from the tub to the toilet, I managed to get out before Mama came back. I hurried into the bedroom. When Mama came in to get me dressed, she didn't realize that I had gotten out of the tub on my own. Eventually, I told her that I had managed the task of getting out unassisted. This would be a major accomplishment for me, but a frightening realization for my mother.

Shocked, she said, "Do you think that I would have ever realized it? Please don't do that again."

Mama wasn't getting much sleep at night because I was constantly waking up during the night. When she would hear me she would come get into the bed with me. This meant she would be awakened all through the night. The problem was that my skin was extremely sensitive. The whole while that I had been hospitalized, I felt grit underneath my skin. Not being able to brush the bed off myself, I tried to explain to other people where the grit was on the sheets. Now that I was able to use my arms again I was constantly trying to keep grit off the bed. If anybody was in the bed with me, I would rub under them, trying to remove the grit that was going to move on my side of the bed when they moved, irritating my skin. Mama would tell me to get up so she could shake the sheets. This didn't eliminate the problem. This pattern continued for years, and still today there are times when I have to rub the grit from the bed.

The visitors had stopped coming long before I left the hospital. Once I was home, the visitors remained infrequent. Some members of my immediate family never came to see me. My grandfather would come to see me only once, after my return home. My sister was one of his favorite grandchildren, and between the two of us it wasn't even a close competition for his affection. Usually, when he came by the house, he would call my sister, Crystal, and have her to meet him outside at his car. There, he would give her money.

I had been the "Black Sheep" of the family for years. It was apparent that something was wrong between them. He only called me whenever she was at school. One day, he came by the house to see me, having called before he came by. He told me that I had married "Trash." According to him, this was why I had been burned. There were a lot of rumors about what had happened to me, but this was the most memorable. Rather than dwell on those who didn't care enough to come see me, I drew closer to God. I was thankful for those who God touched to show me compassion.

When I told Crystal what Mr. Russell had said to me, she told me this was why she had cursed him out. She had cursed him out during the period when they thought that I was dying. She was sure that they were only visiting me to appease their consciences before I died. Crystal also told me what had happened between them.

"He begged me not to be like you. He told me that if I went to college, he would help pay for it. I didn't appreciate him talking about you, so I cursed him out."

Perhaps, some members of my family would have been more relieved if I had died. At least, I would no longer be able to bring shame on the family name.

My Aunt Bobbie would come down sometimes. Now remember, Earline and Aunt Bobbie were "Beer Buddies." Earline had committed her life to God, and she no longer drank beer. Whenever Bobbie came to town, she would stay up all night talking to Mama. One night while they were doing this Earline woke up. She had a message from heaven for Bobbie. With boldness of the Apostle Paul she delivered the message.

"Aunt Bobbie you need to stop drinking beer, and you need to stop messing with that deacon. He's a deacon in the church and he has no business messing with you. You need to give your life to Jesus. I don't mean just going to church. You need to live right."

Aunt Bobbie in her usual form responded, "But Earline, I need somebody to take care of me and somebody to hold me."

Earline responded with conviction, "You have a job. You can take care of yourself, and God will hold you."

The answer from Aunt Bobbie came back, "Well Earline, I have one beer left up to Mae's (Bobbie's mother) house, after I drink that one, I'll stop drinking."

Before she went back off to sleep, Earline told her, "Pour it out or whatever you need to do but don't drink it."

Earline was about five years old during this exchange. Aunt Bobbie drank other beers, but she said she didn't drink that one, and she gave up the deacon. Years later, she quit drinking for good.

Earline also entertained us with her reading skills. Ma'Dear had read some stories to Earline so many times that she had memorized the stories. She had also memorized when to turn the pages. She put lots of emotions into her reading. Mama had a friend to stop by one day, and we told her to let Earline read her a story. She was supposed to read along silently with Earline. When Earline finished the routine, the lady was amazed at how well Earline could read. We tried to tell her that this was a joke, but she wouldn't believe us. She told us that we were mistaken; the child could read.

Soon, I would gather enough strength to begin driving. There was a strategic problem; I wasn't strong enough to open the door. Someone else would need to open the door, so I would stand there until someone passed by to let me in or out of the car. Eventually, I was able to open the door by placing both of my feet against the door and pushing. There were so many things that I had taken for granted. The things we sometimes refer to as small things were now major accomplishments for me. It bothered me to hear anybody say, "I thank God for the small things." Being able to brush my own teeth was a major accomplishment. I had longed to do this the whole time that I was in the hospital.

We rubbed Coca Butter on my skin constantly after I was burned. During the early days, we were only able to apply this to my face and ears. Later, we were able to apply the cocoa butter to the rest of my body. My face, lips, and ears healed almost normally. The color returned to my skin. The scars are still there but most of them healed flat. My hair grew back very quickly and it was thicker and healthier than it was before it was burned.

The process for me to begin receiving my disability had been started at the hospital, but my claim was denied several times. An attorney from Georgia Legal Services helped me with an appeal. This process would be repeated several times and span over a year. Finally, I was granted a hearing before a federal judge. My mother and attorney accompanied me to the hearing. We were required to wait outside of the hearing room. After a short wait, the judge walked out and asked me to come into the room. When we entered the room, he turned to me and gave me instructions.

"You have suffered enough. There is no question about your disability. When the claim was first received the severity of the disability was obvious. If you had gone back to work before a year was up, the claim wouldn't have been paid. I want you to go back into the hall, and when I call you back in, I'm going to record the conversation. This is how you should respond to each of my questions..."

We left the room and returned to the hall. When I was called in the second time, I did according to his instructions. This time the claim was approved. I received a lump sum payment to cover the months that I had been waiting for the claim to be approved. After I began receiving my disability check, I would never have to go for another review. When I received the payment from my disability claim, I spent it within 24 hours. I purchased a car, filled it up with gas, and bought three fish dinners from Earline's favorite restaurant, Captain D's.

Getting another car had been my dream for almost two years. My last car had been repossessed while I was in the hospital, with less than two payments remaining on the car. This had broken my heart. The bank had called me at the hospital stating that it was an emergency that they talk to me. There were no telephones in the rooms on the burn unit. Somehow, they managed to roll me into the hall for the telephone call. When I found out who was calling and why, I couldn't really respond. It was a painful process to move me and usually I tried to get something for pain at least fifteen minutes before I had to be moved. This gave the medication time to get in my system. With this move, I was unable to have the luxury of my medication before being moved. I don't know how they found out that I was in the hospital, and the customer service representative seemed to have no concern for my condition. She was only concerned about the huge amount of money I owed the bank, approximately $120.

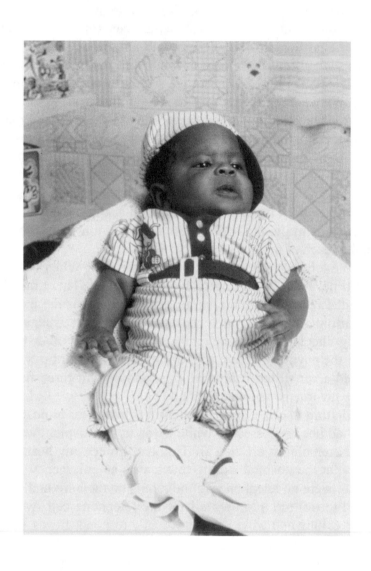

Herman Alexander Hall
God still works miracles.

ZEAL WITHOUT KNOWLEDGE

For I bare them record that they have a zeal of God but not according to knowledge.

Even while in the hospital, from within me, there was a cry, "God you've done so much for me, and I just want to please you." My greatest desire in returning home was to be able to attend regular church services. While in the hospital, I watched the television evangelists, mostly Fred Price, but I had a deeper desire within me.

As the hart panteth after the water brooks, so panteth my soul after thee, O God. My soul thirsteth for God, for the Living God.
Psalm 42:1-2a

When God had come into my life at the hospital, I was instantly delivered from profanity, marijuana, adultery, and even my desire for the streets. There were other things that I had been delivered from but these were my obvious sins. Although, I had received no teaching on defiling the body, my understanding was clear in this area. I understood that these things weren't pleasing to God, and I needed to stop these habits.

The night is far spent, and the day at hand: let us therefore cast off the works of darkness, and let us put on the armour of light. Let us walk honestly, as in the day: not in rioting and drunkenness, not in chambering and wantonness, not in strife and envying. But put ye on the Lord Jesus Christ, and make not provision for the flesh, to fulfill the lusts thereof. Romans 13:14

Realizing how much I owed Jesus, I wanted to give Him more than I had given the devil. This was a huge task; I had given the devil a lot. My mother was active in Sunday School and Bible study. Faithfully, I would begin attending both of these services. As I was learning more about the Word of God, I wanted to be sure that I was in compliance in every aspect of my life. My mother was still the only person that knew what actually happened to me. Lessons about marriage would be taught, periodically. Without fail, being careful not to give away my situation, I would ask if a person does this… is that still your spouse? Unhesitatingly each time, the answer would come back yes. This troubled me for almost two years. There was no contact with my husband during this period, but I was willing to do whatever God required of me.

Most of my strength had returned, with the exception of the physical challenges that would endure long-term. My recovery had reached the point where I was able to move into my own apartment. The apartment was located in an area that was highly infested with drug activity. Eventually, my husband would come to Columbus with Kate, the woman that he was living with at the time that I was burned. My forgiveness of him had been immediate, after the accident, so unforgiveness wasn't a problem. However, the fact that I had already forgiven him left the door open for trying again to make the marriage work. He moved back to Columbus, bringing all of his negative habits with him. This was the same abusive cycle all over again. Additionally, when I would return from church, he would be drunk and angry, often playing gospel music. He appeared to be taunting me for my faith in God.

> *Can a woman forget her suckling child, that she should not have compassion on the son of her womb? Yea, they may forget yet will I not forget thee. Behold, I have graven thee upon the palm of my hands; thou walls are continually before me.* Isaiah 49:15-16

During this time another tragedy occurred in my family. From deep within me there had always been a longing for a real relationship with my father's parents. Somehow, I felt this would link me to my father, providing a measure of completeness in my life. This would never happen. To me my grandparents were known as Mr. Russell and Ms. Beatrice. I didn't know either one of them well enough to address them as "Grandma" or "Granddaddy" or any other title of endearment. Rather than disrespect them, whenever I talked to either one of them, I would just start the sentence, without preceding it with a title. There was one thing that I understood; I hadn't lived up to their expectation. Although, we lived in the same city most of my life, there had been virtually no contact with either of them. My grandmother never came to see me or even called me, during my recovery from the burns. She was about ten blocks away.

One night, my Uncle Glenn was fatally shot in the new McDonald's on Victory Drive. Glenn was what could be referred to as my kind uncle, wild and full of life. This would stimulate a kind turning point in my relationship with my grandmother. This was my grandmother's youngest son and the second son that she lost to a murderer. My heart went out to her, and disregarding my discomfort with going to my own grandmother's house, I went to comfort her. This was like going to a stranger's house to comfort a stranger. This may have been the first time that she had seen me since I had been burned. I'm not sure. Anyway, she was almost inconsolable. Yet, in spite of our relationship or the lack there of, she seemed to find a measure of comfort in my being there. I would like to think that in my being there, she found a small attachment to the other son that she had lost, my father.

She never told me why, but she almost seemed to need me at this time in her life. After my uncle was buried, my intentions were to help her in any way that I could. This would be in spite of personal pain to me. There would be constant reminders that I was one of the "Black Sheep" in the family. In the beginning, I took her to visit Glenn's grave almost daily. We planted sod on his grave, and took gallons of water to the cemetery to water the grass.

She had several insurance policies on Glenn. When these policies paid off, she shared the proceeds with her children and grandchildren. This included my sister and me. Although my sister is the mirror image of one of my father's sisters, my grandmother seldom called her name. This was because my mother was two months pregnant with my sister when my father died. My grandmother doubted that he was my sister's father before she was born. Once Crystal was born all doubt was removed. Crystal bares no resemblance to my mother or me. This didn't change anything for our grandmother, but this seemed to make our grandfather love Crystal more than me, because she was the mirror image of one his daughters.

My grandmother gave me one hundred dollars, and told me to tell Crystal to come by her house so that she could give her a hundred dollars. When Crystal went by she gave her fifty dollars. This in and of itself wasn't the problem; we didn't expect anything. She had never given us anything before, and there was no need for us to expect anything at this time. What hurt me the most was that she told how good she was to her grandchildren and what she had given them. Was I her grandchild? Or was there something I had missed. Was Crystal holding back on me? This didn't include Crystal and me, and this didn't include my Uncle Wallace's daughter, Cookie (Rhonda). Cookie was also a "Black Sheep" in the family.

Additionally, my grandmother told me what she had given each of her children. This included "My Uncle Wallace," as my grandmother called him. This was because he was another Black Sheep. Actually, there were so many of us that could wear this title, if the truth was known, that there should have been no distinction. I knew quite a bit of this truth. Now back to my Uncle Wallace. My grandmother decided to handle him differently.

"I'm not going to give him any of my money to spend on women. Take me to the post office and I'll get money orders to pay his bills."

Maybe she didn't know this, but I knew him well enough to know that if he wanted the cash money, he would find a way to cash them.

My grandmother began to call me regularly to ask me to take her on errands. Each time, she would tell me about whomever she had done something for. She would continuously tell me, "I'm a good mother. I'm good to my children and grandchildren." I listened in silence with my pain. We went to the grocery store several times a week. This was a real experience. In each of the four corners of the buggy, my grandmother would place groceries for various people in our family. Nobody was asking for the groceries. This was just something that she wanted to do. Wallace and I were included in the corners. Our corners contained chicken leg quarters, ground beef, chicken wieners, and hens. The other corners contained chicken breast or wings, ground chuck, steaks, and jumbo beef wieners. Additionally, when she bought cereal for some of my younger cousins, she would check the prices of the cereals. She would buy my cousins the most expensive kinds of cereal. She bought my children generic cereal. I kept my tears locked inside, never telling her that my children ate name brand cereal and I didn't like chicken thighs.

My granddaddy was another story. Both of my grandparents were now married to other people, but they had a lot in common. I'll be nice and not speak ill of the dead. I'll let their own words speak for them. One day, I went by to see my grandfather. The following conversation ensued.

"Charlotte when are you going to do something with yourself?"

I didn't acknowledge the question because this implied that I hadn't done anything with my life.

He proceeded, "Don't you want a college education? All of your aunts went to college."

Adamantly I responded, "No sir."

Trying to prove his point, "Don't you want a new car and house?"

Again I responded, "No sir."

He became really angry with me, "Why?"

Resolutely I responded, "I would like those things if somebody else gave them to me or paid for them. Personally, I don't want to pay for a house for twenty years."

His wife came to my rescue, "Bo calm down. Everybody doesn't want the same things."

There was however one lesson that I learned from Mr. Russell. One day when I went by to see him, he asked me if I had bought Earline's Easter dress. I told him that I hadn't bought anything yet. He said he wanted to buy her something, since he had only given her something once. When Earline was born, he had given me a portable crib from his family. He asked his wife to take me to Kiddie Shoppe to get Earline a dress.

These were his instructions, "Don't buy the most expensive dress in the store and don't buy the cheapest."

This is something that I usually practice now. When we got to the store, I picked out a dress for Earline, and Ms. Annie Pearl picked out another one. She bought Earline two beautiful dresses, without worrying about the price. The one she bought was the most beautiful in the store and the most expensive.

Ms. Beatrice called me several times each day. During these conversations she told me about everything she did for everybody, including paying car notes, paying house notes, day care fees, charge card bills, buying televisions, etc. After this she would make a declaration.

"I'm good to my children and grandchildren. I'm a good mother."

Once my lights were endanger of being disconnected. This took everything in me to humble myself to the point of asking for her help. We were in my car and I had just taken her to pay bills for someone that she was "always good to." When I got the nerve to ask, I made sure she couldn't see my face.

"I hope somebody will be able to help you."

I had asked for an enormous sum of $50. The next day she told me again about how much money she was spending being a good mother and grandmother.

And she conceived, and bare a son; and said, God has taken away my reproach. Genesis 30:23

Within a few months of my reconciling with Robert, I would realize that I had again made a dreadful mistake. My questions concerning marriage relationships escalated. The answers to my questions came back the same each time.

"Marriage is a permanent covenant. Christians are suppose to win the unsaved spouse."

With the emotional and physical abuse that continued, it was hard for me to reconcile the God who had forgiven me for all my wretchedness, with the one that wouldn't forgive me choosing the wrong spouse. Slowly, I began to feel isolated within the church. There was no one who understood the misery that I was going through. Of course, I hadn't told anybody but my mother what had caused the accident that had changed my life forever. Although, I continued to faithfully attend services, I was moving further from a God that was punishing me for marrying this horribly brutal man.

With everything within me, I was trying to live up to what I thought God expected of me. Without a doubt, I was failing to achieve these false expectations. It was apparent that either he was going to kill me or I was going to kill him. Once I made up my mind to put him out permanently, I felt like a complete failure as a Christian.

> *Your words have been stout against me, saith the Lord. Yet ye say, What have we spoken so much against thee? Ye have said, It is in vain to serve God: and what profit is it that we have kept his ordinance, and that we have walked mournfully before the Lord of host?* Malachi 3: 13-14

To make matters even more complicated. God was about to perform a miracle in my body. My daughter was the only child, only grandchild, and only great-grandchild. However, at the age of five, she had committed her life to God. Within her God had placed a love for His word and for prayer. At age seven, she had begun to pray for a miracle, she was lonely and tired of being the only child. She prayed for her mother to become pregnant. Considering the totality of the problems that I had with my body, I thought this was utterly impossible. To my astonishment, God granted her request, and I conceived after I had decided to end the marriage and had asked Robert to move out.

Most of the skin covering my body was extremely tight, particularly in my abdominal area and my chest was still flat. My plastic surgeries had never been completed. After returning to Grady for two additional operations, I became too frightened to have the other surgeries. Each time that I was released from the hospital, the doctors would explain which procedures they would perform when I returned for the next operation. This gave me time mentally to prepare for the operations. However, when I had gone in for the last surgery, instead of operating on one spot, they decided they would complete three areas. I was prepared for them to operate on one spot, but this scared me. When I learned this, I panicked. My mother had already left for the bus ride back to Columbus. By the time she arrived home, I was on the telephone begging her to catch the next bus back to the hospital. To add to my fear, my roommate was having cosmetic surgery on the same area for the third time. The surgeries were only providing limited results. She told me that eventually the implants would begin to sag. I decided to forget the additional operations, choosing to make that operation my last operation.

In spite of my pregnancy, the physical abuse continued. Perhaps, the brutality and frequency of the beatings got worse. Robert began knocking me down routinely. Once, he was trying so hard to hit me that he ran into a brick wall, causing a gash in his head. He was drunk again. Although I didn't realize this at the time, God was truly protecting my child and me from his abuse. Robert and I were separated, but we saw each other occasionally, and most of our interactions were violent. He was living with his mother in a nearby neighborhood.

There were very few problems with my pregnancy, and my tight skin stretched without ripping. In some ways it seemed that the pregnancy was designed to stretch my skin and aid my ability to stand erect. This pregnancy was totally different than my pregnancy with Earline. Whenever, the baby moved you could see his foot or fist protruding from my stomach. It seemed as if he was playing football inside of me for most of the pregnancy.

Blessed shall be the fruit of thy body, and the fruit of thy ground, and the fruit of thy cattle, the increase of thy kine, and the flocks of thy sheep. Blessed shall be thy basket and thy store.
Deuteronomy 28:4-5

On January 3, 1983, after twenty-three hours of labor, I gave birth to a healthy baby boy, Herman Alexander Hall. He was named after my father and my grandmother. This was my miracle baby. When my son was born, Robert and I were still separated. Still trying to reconcile my conflicting views of God, I continued to try to make the marriage work. However, the lengths of our reconciliations were lasting less than a week, more like one to two days. There were two of these attempts, each resulted in an additional pregnancy. Both of these were ectopic pregnancies. The babies were lodged in my fallopian tubes. Both tubes were removed within a six-month time period. Herman would be my last child.

Herman was special from the beginning. We never forgot that he was my miracle child. He gave us lots of reminders. The pregnancy had helped some of the physical problems in my body. My skin wasn't nearly as tight, and clothes weren't quite as irritating to my skin. It was easier for me to stand almost erect. I wanted to breast feed my baby, and God blessed my chest just enough to perform the task. However, this area was still far short of normal.

When Herman was almost seven months old, I placed him in the floor on a blanket. I went outside to hang up clothes. When I returned, he was standing at the living room table. A week later, Herman began walking. By the time he was a year old, he had a very large vocabulary of words. By the time he was eighteen months, he could easily carry on a conversation.

There was a habit that he developed early; this habit would be very hard for him to break. He preferred to slip off, rather than ask permission.

Blessed shall be the fruit of thy body, and the fruit of thy ground, and the fruit of thy cattle, the increase of thy kine, and the flocks of thy sheep. Blessed shall be thy basket and thy store.
Deuteronomy 28:4-5

In spite of this miracle child, the relationship with Robert was getting worse. There had been numerous attempts to reconcile the problems in the marriage, but each time the abuse would return. What had I done to deserve this awful and abusive marriage? Why wouldn't God forgive me for making this terrible mistake? He had forgiven me for everything else that I had done, things far worse. The punishment was more severe than I could tolerate. The teachings that I received were conflicting with my view of a loving, forgiving God. I was determined to put Robert out of my house, and out of my life. Somebody had to understand what I was going through. Returning to what was familiar, I started visiting my friends in the streets. These visits started out as weekly visits after I left church each Sunday, feeling empty, lonely, confused, and hurt. Robert would be with his family, getting drunk, listening to gospel music and dancing. Getting high was still not appealing to me. However, in my mind, I had already failed God miserably. In my confusion, I was already a backslider because I had made up my mind, I was going to divorce Robert or kill him, to avoid him killing me. Based on the strict teaching that I had received, I was a failure at being saved.

Financially, I was struggling, and needed to come up with a way to produce additional income. My neighbors would ask me to take them to pay their bills or to the grocery store. For these services, they gave me small amounts of money that enabled me to keep gas in my car. Whenever I took them to the grocery store, I would help them stretch their money by picking the best bargains. I enjoyed doing these things, but I really wasn't making enough money to live comfortably.

If I understood anything, it was the effects of marijuana. Anyone smoking the drug would be prone to sudden increases in appetite. I decided to capitalize on the drug traffic in the neighborhood. The children would name me hot-dog Lady. Making hot-dogs with homemade chili was one of my specialties. I decide to put this skill to work. Passing out samples of my hot-dogs to the people selling drugs on the corner kicked my business off. I began selling hot-dogs, sodas, and cupcakes. Later, I began selling dinners on Sundays. Some children in the neighborhood began buying hot-dogs for breakfast, and this concerned me. After questioning them, it would become apparent that the utilities were off at their house. I would ask them to take me to their apartment to meet their parents. Whenever possible, I would do what I could to assist them with getting the utilities turned back on. This meant begging churches and non-profit agencies for help. I never stopped begging until I reached my goal, and their utilities were reconnected.

The hot-dog business was going good, and providing the extra income that I needed. Some thought my business was going too well. The owners of a restaurant on the corner of Alpine Drive called the Health Department twice after my business began interfering with their business. Each time the Health Department came out to investigate, I wasn't home. They left a message in the front door for me to call the Health Department. These were courtesy calls to inform me of the complaints, because they said they could find no evidence that I was selling hot-dogs.

Charlotte R. Hall
Where is your faith?

AND THE HOUSE WAS EMPTY

Then goeth he, and taketh with him seven other spirits more wicked than himself, and they enter in to dwell there: and the last state of the man is more worse than the first.

My visits to my friends in the street became more frequent and lasted longer because my guilt was increasing. Each time that I went, the drugs were abundantly available to me, but I refused to indulge. Whenever someone would offer me a joint or a beer, my friend Reba would speak up, telling him or her that I was saved. However, the joy of my salvation was dwindling fast. This was being replaced with pain, confusion, and frustration.

When He the Spirit of truth comes, he will guide you into all truth. He will not be presenting his own ideas; he will be telling you what he has heard. He will tell you about the future. John 16:13 NLT

My marriage left no room for joy or love. I didn't have what I needed to rightly divide the "Word of Truth," (the Bible). The Baptism of Holy Ghost was what I needed to help me discern the truth. For two years, I had been seeking the Baptism of Holy Ghost, but hadn't received this gift. Perhaps because I was trying to earn the free gift of God. I would never be able to earn God's favor.

And I say unto you, Ask, and it shall be given you: seek, and ye shall find; knock and it shall be opened unto you. for everyone that asketh receiveth; and he that seeketh findeth; and to him that knocketh it shall be opened. If a son shall ask bread of any of you that is a father, will he give him a stone? Or if he ask a fish, will he for a fish give him a serpent? Or if he shall ask an egg, will he offer a scorpion? If ye then, being evil, know how to give good gifts unto your children: how much more shall your heavenly Father give the Holy Spirit to them that ask him? Luke 11:9-13

One day while I was sitting at my friend's house, feeling sorry for myself, someone offered me a joint. Normally my friend Reba would answer.

"No. Charlotte's saved."

Before she could answer this time, I said that I wanted the joint. The demons were waiting on me to miss a beat.

When an unclean spirit is gone from out of a man: he walketh around through dry places, seeking rest; and finding none, he saith,

I will return unto the house whence I came out. And when he cometh, he findeth it swept and garnished. Then goeth he and taketh to him seven other spirits more wicked than himself; and they enter in, and dwell there: and the last state of the man is worse than the first.
Luke 11:24-26

With one puff, every demon that I had been delivered from returned bringing company. Immediately, I took a beer to go with the joint. Shortly, after Herman turned seven months old, I stopped going to church. Before the week was out I was smoking drugs like I had never stopped. I was smoking marijuana between my hot-dog sales. My regular customers were allowed to purchase hot-dogs on credit. The first of each month, I collected the debts. There were large wine bottles that I used to save dimes, nickels, and pennies, a separate jar for each one. This was because I had heard a story of a man who saved enough pennies for his daughter to go to college. These were my savings for Earline.

During the first week of the month, I would have to leave my business to pickup Herman's WIC (food vouchers provided under the Women Infants and Children Program). In the kitchen of my apartment there was a black wrought iron baker's rack sitting in front of the window. This was stacked with a variety of name brand cereals. When I returned from picking up the WIC, boxes of cereal were scattered across the kitchen floor. Alpine was a high crime area; therefore, I knew immediately that someone had broken into my apartment. Going directly to my bedroom, I went to the drawer that housed the money that I had collected that week. I hadn't taken time to deposit the money into the bank. The money was gone from its hiding place. Returning to the kitchen for further inspection, I discovered that glass was all over the floor. Opening the back door, I went out into the back yard. Dimes were everywhere. When I returned to the house, a jar of nickels and a jar of dimes were missing. I called the police, but before they could get to the apartment, I went walking up and down Alpine angrily looking for the culprit. I was walking so fast that one of neighbors warned me.

"Baby, slow down. Please don't fall."

It took me all of five minutes to find out who had stolen my money. Al was one of my "Smoking Buddies."

When the children in the neighborhood returned home from the school, Al's niece agreed to show me where he stayed, in a nearby neighborhood. I had all the details of the burglary now. He had been waiting until I left home that morning. People were always standing around on

Alpine, but their presence didn't deter him. He had thrust the handle of my mop through the window in the back door to gain entry into the apartment. When he returned from within the house, he jumped the fence in the backyard. In his haste he broke the jar of dimes. When we got to Al's house no one was home. I provided this information to the police. The police were unable to locate him even with having his address.

A month later, I was at the WIC clinic again, in came Al's wife. Remaining calm, I went directly to my car, trying to quickly spot Al. He was standing outside a short distance from their car. When he saw me, he didn't have enough time to make it to the car. Immediately, I was fuming with anger again. He took off running up the street with me hot on his trail. He ran back and forth across the street trying to shake me off his trail. Determined to hit him with the car, I drove the same way, darting in and out between the cars driving down the road. The more he ran the more engulfed I became with anger. Finally, he left the main road, jumping several fences and running through backyards of nearby houses. A few months later, he beat his wife, and she had him arrested. The warrant was served for him breaking in my house. He pleaded guilty and was sentenced to prison. Several years later, I saw him working as a trustee (prisoner allowed to work outside of the prison). Smiling he walked over to me.

"You wouldn't believe how many times I've violated the sentence that I got for breaking in your house. I'm in here on it again."

I smiled, glad I hadn't hit him with the car.

Herman knew everyone in the neighborhood who woke up early in the mornings, and everyone who drank coffee. Herman loved coffee, which I seldom made. This was something that he got from Ma'Dear, not from me. When he was about a year old, this would get him in trouble. Upon arriving home one night he requested a cup of coffee. The weather was cold, so I decided to immediately prepare the coffee. Herman stopped next door to speak to our neighbor before coming in the house. After I prepared the cup of coffee, I placed this on the washing machine. Herman ran in the house grabbing the cup of coffee, while I was getting him an ice cube from the freezer to cool the coffee. He turned the cup of coffee over before I could stop him. Herman's wrist was burned, but the jacket that he was wearing protected him from extensive injury. He was never big on crying and this would be no exception. This may also have been because Earline was crying and screaming hysterically.

"Oh God don't let my brother die. This is my only brother."

She screamed this all the way to the hospital. I've never thought about this before now, but perhaps she was having a flash back to the time when I had been burned. When we arrived at the hospital, the nurse made an excuse to send me back to the front desk. This was to allow her time to question Earline about Herman's accident. When she asked Earline what had happened to Herman. Earline understood the implications and responded.

"Ask him. He can talk."

Herman explained to the nurse how he had been burned. When I walked back into the room the nurse was finishing her questions.

She said to him, "I bet you don't want any more coffee."

To this statement he responded, "I'm going to get me a cup as soon as I get home."

Later, I renewed my relationship with Jim when he returned again to Columbus. Whereas, I smoked a half of an ounce of marijuana a week before, this was my daily allotment. Before, I had only snorted cocaine a couple of times. This time, I would develop a love for sniffing cocaine, and for the freeze that came from licking the cocaine bags. Other habits were on the way. My love for the nightclubs didn't return, but hanging out there occasionally, went with the lifestyle.

Jim still had his same bad habits and I really didn't have the patience to deal with a lot of this foolishness anymore. He had always had the upper hand before, but that was going to change this time. Every time he crossed me, I was going to strike back. Whenever he would cut his dope, I would watch to see what he dropped, or what he miscounted. This was something that I had worked out with his sister, Reba. Between the two of us, we caught him slipping quite often. He was so sure that he had me wrapped around his fingers and he didn't think I would ever steal from him. He was sure that his money was coming up short, but he couldn't pinpoint where the loss was occurring. One day, he asked me if I thought his sister would steal from him. I assured him that she wouldn't, he was miscounting.

For most of the time that I had been married, I had been back and forth between relationships with Jim and Robert. Neither one of them was providing what I needed in a relationship. There was still a need within me for someone to love me, just me, just as I was, without stipulations. Neither of these relationships provided this emotional reinforcement. For nearly ten years, I had been accepting less than I wanted in a man and a relationship. This was getting stale. I was tired of settling for less than I wanted. On numerous occasions, I had promised myself that I was finished with both pitiful relationships, only to return to continue the cycle. Actually, I was tired of hearing myself make these empty promises, and no one else believed that I would ever end either pathetic relationship. I had been crying wolf for a long time, but this was about to change. Robert had already pushed me beyond my limits, and Jim, having learned very little about me over the years, was about to make the same mistake. He thought that he would have me wrapped around his finger forever. If you had asked me, I would have told you, he was right.

Jim liked showing off in his usual flamboyant style. He particularly liked to prove that I would do whatever he asked me to do. This had been his sick and selfish pattern for years. Actually, we both knew this was far from the truth. But, knowing this was what he thrived on, I would go along with the game whenever anyone else was present. Most of the time, I never followed through on his request, and he never questioned me about this. Jim and Robert had a few things in common, they are both men that are small in statue, and they both had Napoleon Complexes. Jim's complex just expressed itself in a different style. He needed to prove that he had emotional control over women. During this period, he was really pushing my patience with him to a new limit, constantly flashing his women in my face.

One day, I was at Denna's house sitting on the porch. This was where I went most of the time when I was hanging in the streets. Three guys came up, and asked to speak to her inside the house. Two of the guys were familiar to me. But the third one, I had never seen him before. There was something about him that captured my attention, as no one had in years. Our eyes locked on each other. We made a very thorough and complete observation of each other. We didn't say anything, but man was he fine. After they completed their mission, I asked Denna who he was. She told me his name was Buck. They had stopped by her house to get high. Buck just didn't look the part, and it was hard for me to imagine him as a junkie. He was the best-looking man that I had seen in a long time.

That night I was planning to go to the H & D in Phenix City with Denna, and Jim's sister, Reba. We had all planned to wear red dresses. Jim knew that this was our plan. He had another plan. When Denna and I arrived to pick his sister up, my cousin was there with her boyfriend. Reba informed me that she wasn't going because Jim was planning to take someone else to the same club, and she didn't want to be in the middle of our mess. After I assured her that there would be no trouble, she agreed to go. Before we left the apartment, his date arrived to pick him up. He was sure that this would get a reaction from me. As everybody waited, there was no outward reaction from me, but inside I was fuming. My relationship with Jim always included other women. This wasn't what made me mad. When it came to him hustling or pimping, I didn't have a problem with this. But a date? And without telling me about this. He knew me well enough to know this was sure to get a reaction from me. And I knew him well enough to know this was a setup. He was banking on my response. Not this night. I was determined he wouldn't see me sweat.

I was still more of a marijuana smoker or "Pot Head." At the clubs, I usually drank Coca-Cola. If I felt a need for a buzz, I would go outside and smoke a joint or two. Jim never showed up at the club, but I was really upset, embarrassed, and hurting. No longer able to hold my feelings in, I went outside to my car. Once inside the car, I cried like a fool, and I cried, and I cried. This time I wasn't going back to Robert. After all my tears abated, I dried my face, smoked a joint and returned to the club, ready to move on with the next phase of my life. There was an announcement that I needed to make to Reba and Denna. They had heard this before.

"That's the last time he's going to hurt me."

They weren't impressed with my announcement. In spite of their disbelief, this was the last time that he was able to inflict pain in my heart.

Events began to happen fast inside the club. There were two bars inside the H&D, one when you entered the club and another in the back of the club. As one of the few bars in the area that stayed open to 6:00 a.m., it was usually packed. Tonight was no different. Standing near the rear bar, a friend, Pete asked me if I would do him a favor. He had brought a friend with him to the club, but he was leaving the club early and his friend would need a ride home. As he was attempting to introduce me to his friend standing behind me, I turned around, and for the second time that day it happened. My eyes locked with those of this man.

He said, "This is my friend Buck."

I responded, "I'll be more than glad to drop him off."

Sure, I was more than willing to give him a ride home. Buck asked me to dance. Normally, I would have said no, but tonight was different, I wanted to dance with this man.

Afterwards, I returned to my table with my companions. My mind was no longer with them. My eyes kept locking with this man across the crowded room. I began to have a fantasy. Not that kind, we were in a nightclub, but I was having a heavenly vision. We were in church, this man was going to be my husband. He was up preaching from the pulpit and I was out in the congregation, dancing in the spirit. God was actually far from my mind. I was so shocked by this that I told him. He simply responded that several people had prophesied that he was going to be a preacher. My companions never noticed the sparks that were firing between this man that I had just met and me.

As we drove from the club, Reba sat in the front seat. She was worn out and dropping off to sleep. Denna sat in the back seat with Buck making passes at him. He was sitting directly behind me. In the rear view mirror I kept looking at him and he kept looking at me. We stopped to get something eat, and ran into two other people that we knew. They were looking for something to do and told Denna that they would come by her house. Reba wanted to go home, and I was relieved. She didn't need to be with me for the rest of the night. When everybody arrived at Denna's, the party continued, and so did this gaze between Buck and me. We weren't talking to each other, just looking at each other.

> *Wherein times past ye walked according to the course of this world, according to the prince and power of the air, the spirit that worketh in the children of disobedience: Among whom also we had our conversations in times past in the lust of our flesh, fulfilling the desires of the flesh and the mind; and were by nature the children of wrath, even as others.* Ephesians 2:2-3

Finally, Buck asked me if I wanted to talk to him, and we excused ourselves to one of the bedrooms. And talk we did, about everything. Here we were two strangers exchanging our complete life stories. It was amazing that we had journeyed through all the same cities at opposite times. We knew most of the same people from the streets, but our paths had never crossed. After we finished talking, he asked me to move next to him on the bed. Since we entered the bedroom, I had been sitting in a chair near the bed. I explained to him that I didn't believe in one-night stands. If anything were ever going to happen between us, he would have to be ready for a long-term commitment. A strange thing to tell a stranger, even stranger, he agreed to this. At this time, I was extremely self-conscious of my body, which made everything that was happening even stranger. Taking my clothes off in front of a stranger wasn't one of my repressed fantasies. Whether, it was winter or summer, I always wore turtleneck dickeys, and long sleeves. My scars were confined to places that could be almost completely hidden by my clothes. This was my sign to the world that I didn't want to be asked about the scars. Now remember, my mother was still the only person who knew what had happened to me on the burning bed.

There was now a second person who knew the story. When daylight found us still together, I was shocked by my actions and wanted to hurry home.

We agreed that we would meet at the H & D again that night. However, all day he remained on my mind, and I wanted to see him again. I didn't want to wait until nightfall. Denna and I decided to head to Ninth Street; maybe I would see him. This was a place that I had never hung out before. Usually, when I came through there with Jim, I remained in the car. Jim and Reba were on Ninth Street. He was flirting with everybody, as usual. Patiently, I waited until I saw the vision that I had been anticipating. My memory of him walking down the street is still rather vivid. We confirmed our date for later that night. Still, no one noticed that I was acting totally out of character. A week before, there was no way I would have a private conversation with a man in front of Jim, or would even have stayed on Ninth Street for more than a few minutes.

After we left the club that night, Buck went home with me. He had planned to take the bus back to Atlanta that Sunday afternoon. This is where he was living and working. He planned to return to Columbus the following Friday. Needless to say, he missed the bus. That Sunday night I would drive him back to Atlanta. He was concerned about me driving back to Columbus alone, and asked one of his friends, Willie, to ride to Atlanta with us. The next day, Willie would tell Jim about my trip to Atlanta and my new relationship. This would lead to a minor confrontation between Jim and me. When I saw Jim, I was with Denna. He gave Denna a message to give me.

"Tell that girl if I had known she was taking that nigga' Buck to Atlanta, she could have brought me a package back."

There was no need for her to tell me what he said, since they were both standing next to my car, and I was in the car. I didn't respond. When Denna and I drove around the street to her sister's house, Willie was there, getting high. Jim had given him a sack of dope for the information. In spite of all this, Jim assumed this was something that would pass and that he was still in control. He was wrong, I had cried him out of my system, and my thoughts were now focused on Buck.

That Thursday, Reba, Denna, and I decided to have a barbecue at Denna's apartment. Later that evening, Jim came by. When he walked in, I didn't look up. He demanded that I come outdoors, but I didn't respond. Reba and Denna both jumped up to confront him, telling him that he couldn't make me do anything. He began to raise his voice at them, and I was concerned that he might hit one of them. I didn't think that he would hit me, so I agreed to go outside with him.

During this time, I wore thirteen gold chains around my neck. When I walked outside with him, to my utter dismay, he grabbed all of them, causing several of them to break. After this he told me to come to Reba's house to pick him up. Starring at him, I remained quite. Reba was riding with me and I had to take her home, but I wasn't going to pick him up. Rather than dropping Reba off in front of her house, I dropped her off on the corner near her house. I went home, but I hid my car. I was expecting Buck to come back to see me on the next evening.

All week, I had made plans for a romantic weekend. Well, Friday came and there was no Buck. He didn't have a telephone, so I couldn't call him. Early Saturday morning, I drove to Atlanta to clarify the future of our relationship. The previous weekend, he had introduced me to one of his neighbors. Rather than knocking on his door this early in the morning, I decided that it would be better if she told him that I was in town. I gave her a note to give him with a number where I could be reached. As she knocked on the door, I waited for his response. Trying to hide his shock, he asked me into his apartment. I only had one question.

"Are you glad to see me?"

He responded, "I'm shocked, but I'm glad."

He started packing his clothes for Columbus. The next time that he returned here, it would be to pick up the rest of his belongings, completing his move to Columbus. That was seventeen years ago.

Evelyn L. Russell
Stead*y under pressure.*

MAMA'S DREAMS

And he dreamed yet another dream.

Mama wasn't happy about any of this, with the exception of my ending the relationship with Robert. She was constantly concerned about what I was doing. For me, this was hard for me to understand, why she wouldn't accept the way that I had decided to live my life. In my efforts to respect my mother, I always tried to keep my illegal activities away from her. During the time that I had been struggling with the issues in the marriage, she was new in her walk with the Lord. She had been very careful about advising me, not wanting to give me the wrong advice. This was going to change when I picked up my new habits. She began to dream about these habits, and she wasn't about to reserve her opinions.

There had been times when I was in New York that I had picked pockets or took advantage of someone, but for the most part this wasn't my hustle. This had been a habit that I picked up from a seventeen-year-old girl from Alabama. She told me that she started stealing at an early age. She started out by stealing from her mother. We would walk through the business district in downtown New York looking for easy prey. If we spotted a man in a business suit with a look of lust in his eyes, we would approach him. We would talk to him like he was just irresistible, as she eased her hands into his pockets. Sometimes, Good Samaritans passing by would intervene. This happened on one occasion when we had walked off with a man's wallet. A Good Samaritan walked up on us and made us give the wallet back to him. We had walked away without the man missing his wallet.

On one occasion, we met a man who had too much money in his pocket. Rather than peeling off part of the money, she tried to remove the whole roll from his pocket. This roll was too thick for her to remove from his pockets with two fingers The wind was blowing, and when she pulled the roll out, money was flying all over the street. The three (including the man) of us were all on the ground, trying to grab whatever we could. We flagged a cab down, and jumped in while he was still trying to catch the rest of his money. We gave the cab driver a good tip for picking us up.

Now, I was involved with another kind of thief, a real thief. This was a new habit that I would pick up. Shopping was what I did best, and shoplifting was what he did best. Five minutes in a store and I could spot the most expensive items in the store. This would be my new job, spotting the items, or moving them all to one location in the store, earning me a cut of the profits and one of each outfit. By one of each outfit, I mean that I wanted one in every color and each style. The other people on the team took turns removing the items from the store. Buck's favorite thing was trashing the stores. By this process, he was able to lift all of the clothes from the rack with one swift movement, and with the precision of a surgeon, roll the items together, and place them in a garbage bag. After he made his way to the outside of store, he carried the bag as if it was trash.

Buck had a drug addiction that was driving his stealing. Mine was an addiction to clothes. I drank champagne everyday and smoked marijuana like it was a cigarette. When I purchased the marijuana, I would clean the seeds from all of it, roll all of it, and place them in a box next to my bed. There were always joints next to my bed. After all, I was constantly smoking, one joint behind the other, looking for something that I didn't have. I wanted to be happy, and marijuana made me laugh. This didn't make me happy, but laughing was a close second.

Mama would begin to call me, warning me to stop the things that I was doing. She would tell me that God had shown her what I was doing. To avoid disrespecting her, I would lay the telephone down. Occasionally, I would pick up the telephone to see if she was still talking. Every now and then, I would make a very brief comment, "Uh huh." This was just to make her think that I was listening to her. She would continue trying to warn me, but I wasn't listening. She continued to call every night, with her warnings. This was to no avail since most of the time, the telephone was lying on the bed.

Every day, we dressed to go to work, wearing expensive clothes. Each night, we planned where we would be working the next day, stealing. We would travel out of town to steal. The pay was excellent, our parts averaging five hundred to a thousand dollars a day. The hours weren't bad either. The stress was horrible; I was constantly worrying that we would get caught. This feeling usually came on after we left the store. I was never scared in the process of committing the crimes. The panic hit me after we left the stores, but by the next morning the fear would be gone. Usually, by noon each day, we had enough goods to reach our daily quota.

A couple of months into the relationship, we would get arrested and charged with approximately twelve counts of shoplifting. This is an approximation, because after we were released on bond, the police continued to add on additional charges. When we were arrested, we didn't have any merchandise on us. The owner of one of the shops had identified us as stealing something from his store. The police decide to detain us, mostly because they knew Buck's reputation. They placed a hold on us to prevent us from making bond. Later that evening, the police found an abandoned car downtown. The car was registered to me.

The car was full of items that we had accumulated over several days. Through a process that could only be called guesswork, they attempted to identify where these items came from. There were no identifying labels on any of the items. We were charged with even stealing items that we had purchased. This went on for two days, and finally my lawyer was able to get the hold dropped. Once I was released on bond, I arranged for Buck's release. Frustrated with trying to identify one of the more costly items, a pair of brass bookends with a marble base, the detectives agreed to stop searching for charges, if I would tell them where these came from. To stop the process, I provided the information.

All of the charges were eventually lumped together, for the plea bargain. Buck would claim responsibility for the crimes. Later, he would be sentenced to prison and I would be placed on probation. I was also required to serve two weeks in jail. During these two weeks, I only ate the rolls. I wasn't accustomed to eating food that I didn't like and I wasn't trying to develop a taste for anything I considered unappealing. The judge gave me credit for the days that I served in jail during the arrest process. On the day that I was to be released, there was no record of this arrangement. Worried, I contacted my lawyer. I didn't want to stay in jail one day longer than I had to. My lawyer was able to clear the confusion up. When I was released, I walked to my grandmother's house. I couldn't stand the thought of waiting at the jail for someone to pick me up. I was sick to my stomach for several days, a result of my jailhouse diet.

When I reported to my probation officer, he added an additional requirement to the terms of my probation. He couldn't require me to work because of my physical disability; therefore, he decided to send me to substance abuse treatment. Even after I explained to him that all I used was marijuana, he insisted that I go several times a week. He made the arrangements and I enrolled in the program. After I went to the program a couple of times, I knew I was in the wrong place. Their focus was on heroin and cocaine addiction. I called my lawyer to get me out of this situation. The probation officer angrily agreed that I hadn't been required to attend substance abuse treatment. He had one thing to say.

"If she ever gets in trouble for drugs, I'm going to violate her probation."

Since Buck had confessed to the charges, I felt obligated to support him financially and physically during his incarceration. This meant that I was going to support him by sending him money orders regularly and visiting him at least once a week. Buck was sent to Hardwick, Georgia after he completed diagnostic assessment in Jackson, Georgia. Jackson was a maximum-security prison and the diagnostic screening facility for all male prisoners in the state. Visitation there required that you talk through a huge metal screen that resembled the screen on a barbecue pit, just in exaggerated proportions.

Hardwick, Georgia was approximately thirty miles from Macon. You were only allowed to visit on a Saturday or a Sunday, not both days. It had been a long time since I had spent any real time with Buck and I wanted to see him both days. I came up with a plan to fulfill this desire. That weekend, I rented a room at a local motel for the night. That Saturday, I arrived at the prison wearing a wig and sunglasses. In my hand was Buck's sister's birth certificate. My plan included using her name the first day in case my plot was spoiled on the second day. Additionally, I changed my handwriting when I signed in under her name. The first day came off without a hitch. The next day, I arrived without the wig and sunglasses, as myself. Shortly after visitation began, the guards asked me to come outside. They asked me if I had visited Buck the day before. Assuring them that I hadn't, I asked them to check the sign-in roster, and to compare the names and signatures. Knowing that they remembered Buck kissing the other woman, I explained that she probably had been drinking, and this made her overly affectionate. Not being able to prove otherwise, they let me return to visitation.

A huge fence surrounded Rivers Correctional Facility. Inside the fence, the prison was separated into four separate buildings, each having their own separate visitation room. The seats in the room resembled church pews. One guard was stationed at the front of the visitation room. The other officers remained outside during most of the visitation period. Since I was visiting each Saturday, some of the guards knew me by name. I was observing them too. Believing that there was corruption in everything, I was waiting to catch them slipping on the job, and catch them I would.

One Saturday, one of the officers was struggling to stay awake. This went on throughout the visitation period of about five hours. To make sure the officer knew that I had caught him sleeping, I winked at him. I nicknamed him Sleepy, but I was careful to assure that Buck was the only person that knew what I had on him. Whenever I went to see Buck, I always carried money. One day when I went to see Buck, I was the only visitor in this visitation room, and Sleepy was working visitation. He kept walking out of the room leaving us alone. Buck was scared for me to ask him, but Sleepy was in my debt. Against Buck's protests, I called Sleepy over and made him a proposition. I told him that if he left us alone for the rest of the visitation period, I would give him twenty dollars. Sleepy said that he didn't want the money, but he agreed to leave the room for the remainder of our visit. When I walked out the fence after visitation, I heard someone calling my name.

"Charlotte, Charlotte."

I turned to see two guards peeping from a window; one was Sleepy.

"Come back inside the gate."

When I walked back down the walk, Sleepy said, "Drop that on the ground by my car."

He described his car. As I walked back through the gate headed towards the parking lot, I laughed. I had been right, I was sure the corruption existed. I dropped the twenty dollars on the ground by his car.

Things turned sour at Rivers, one Saturday when I went to see Buck. When I pulled up, some of the prisoners were in the windows; they were trying to signal that something was wrong inside the prison. When I got inside, a female guard said that she would have to search another female visitor and me. As I had nothing on me, except $170, I agreed to the search. She was checking for drugs and I didn't have any on me. There were ways to get drugs into the prison. Me walking in with drugs wasn't one of the options. After the search, she asked me to take the money back to the car before proceeding to visitation.

When I left the prison, I was still angry about how I had been treated. That Monday, I reported the incident to the warden at the prison. He told me that he had received a report about this incident stating that I arrived at the prison with $770 on me, and they suspected that I was bringing this money to Buck for him to purchase drugs. When I asked him why I had been allowed to visit if this was the allegation, he couldn't provide me with an answer. He also informed me that I would no longer be allowed to visit Buck. There was no way I was going to be deterred by this action. After I finished talking to him I began making arrangements for Buck to be transferred. Within two weeks, he was transferred to Jack Rutledge State Prison in Columbus. At least, I would no longer have to make the long trips.

For they heard an awesome trumpet blast and a voice and a message so terrible that they begged God to stop speaking.
Hebrew 12:19 NLT

While Buck was in prison, I would go back to selling drugs. Business was going pretty good, that is until Mama started dreaming again. I was starting to resent these dreams that exposed everything that I was trying to hide from her. She called me one night and told me that she had dreamed that I was selling drugs. I assured her that she was severely mistaken. There was no way that I would ever stoop to selling drugs. She insisted on telling me that if I didn't stop what I was doing, I was going to get caught. This warning was familiar to me. This was the same warning that she gave me when I was stealing. This time she was resolutely determined to acquire and maintain my undivided attention.

She said, "The police were searching your house. They were tearing your sofa apart, like they were sure you had the dope in the sofa. They were tearing the foam in the back of the sofa into small pieces."

While I was assuring her that I would never stoop to selling drugs, at the same time, I was down on my knees in front of the sofa. The telephone was in my left hand, and my right hand was reaching into the back of the sofa, pulling the marijuana from my hiding place. The hiding place that no one knew about. That is except God. All I wanted was for her to hurry up and get off the telephone. She repeated her warnings several times, describing each detail of her dream. While she continued to repeat her warnings, it seemed like she was never going to let me get off the telephone.

She continued explaining, over and over, "The police were searching your house for drugs. They were so sure that you had the drugs, they were ripping you sofa to pieces. They were ripping the foam into small pieces."

I was trying to remain calm, but I was afraid that the police would get there before she hung up the telephone. Mama never said anything important only once. If something were really pressing on her mind, she would repeat the message until she got tired. I needed to get the dope out of the house before the police came. Finally, she was finished.

Nervously, I placed the drugs in a jar, rushed out of the house and quickly buried the drugs in the ground. When the next person came to the house requesting a five-dollar package, I suggested that he take all of the drugs I had, and pay me for them later, approximately seventy-five dollars worth of marijuana. This man was someone that I barely knew. That didn't matter; Mama's dream had me scared.

Surely the Lord God will do nothing, but he revealeth his secret unto his servants the prophets. Amos 3:7

All night long, I stayed awake, expecting the police to show up. Needless to say, I never got paid for the drugs, but that didn't matter. At least the police hadn't found the dope. For a few days, I was scared to sell anything. But then, the devil gave me another plan. He talked to me real good, and based on everything that had happened in the past, I was convinced that he was right. He told me that before anything happened to me, God would warn my mother, and she would warn me. All I had to do was find a new place to sell the drugs and avoid talking to my mother. As long as she was unable to talk to me nothing would happen. This would keep me from getting caught selling drugs. This was a perfect plan.

Two weeks after her warning, I went to see Denna. Normally, she had a package of drugs, but currently she didn't have anything.

She said, "Nobody has been bringing anything by for me to sell."

She wanted to do something if I could work it out. She knew where I could get a pound of marijuana. We went to talk to her friend. The guy didn't really know me but he was familiar with my reputation. He was glad to give me the dope on credit. Thus, I set up shop at Denna's apartment. In addition to splitting the profits with her, I was also giving her part of the drugs for recreational use. Too scared to go home with the dope, I would leave the drugs at her house each night, or should I say morning. It was between 3:00 and 4:00 a.m. when I went home each morning. This was long enough to take a nap, change clothes, and get my daughter off to school. All of this because I was afraid to talk to my mother.

My plan was working. Mama hadn't been able to reach me by telephone for awhile. Business was going extremely well. I was able to pay for the marijuana up front, and get a large quantity of cocaine on credit. We were working both businesses. All of my bills were paid off, and I was doing plenty of shopping. I was able to buy my children anything and everything that they wanted. Every day, I smoked as much marijuana as I wanted. Only now, I sprinkled cocaine in my joints. This is called lacing. Sometimes I snorted cocaine, but more than that I liked licking the bags that had contained the cocaine.

My love for licking the cocaine bags irritated my mouth severely. On the left side of my mouth, I developed a toothache that was driving me insane. This can only be described as being on the left side, because I didn't know whether this pain was at the top or bottom of my mouth. Desperate for some relief, I went to the dentist, but I couldn't tell him which tooth was causing the irritation. After thoroughly examining my mouth, the dentist told me that there was a problem area between two of my teeth at the top, and two of them at the bottom. The dentist stated that he needed to know which tooth was giving me the problem before he could proceed. I couldn't help with identifying the problem. My solution was that he should extract both of my teeth at the top and both of them at the bottom.

She obeyed not the voice; she received not correction; she trusted not in the Lord; she drew not near to her God. Zephaniah 3:2

There was only one problem with my thriving business. Now "Something" began to talk to me, regularly. I now called God, "Something." The voice constantly said, "You're going to get caught." Whenever, I told anybody what the voice said, they told me that I was just paranoid because I had been snorting too much cocaine. There were times when I would sit on the train tracks paranoid. I was trying to see if I could locate the police that were watching the house. Sometimes, I would walk over into the woods and frantically bury the dope. Other times, while I was riding down the street, I would sling the dope out the car window in a brown paper bag, just like trash. When someone would come to make a purchase, I would go back to where I had thrown the drugs from the car. Sometimes, I couldn't even locate the bag, but this wouldn't stop from repeating the pattern. Whenever I went to the shopping center, this was always my pattern. And the voice became more frequent and more insistent, "You're going to get caught." There was no doubt in my mind where the voice was coming from, but I wasn't going to admit that I knew the source.

Finally, I told Denna that I was going to stop selling drugs. The fear of getting caught with the drugs had become overwhelming. Denna told me that she had several bills that hadn't been paid for the month. I agreed to get one more package to help her out. For more than a week, our source was out of drugs and we were waiting for him to reup (get a new shipment). We continuously told our customers to check back later, not knowing exactly when we would get the new supply. This went on for several days. There was one regular customer who had requested that I give him a tester when I got the new supply of cocaine. Pete was a good and regular customer and so I agreed. After making several trips that week to pick up the drugs and coming back without them, I was finally able to pick up the package. This was directly against everything going on in my mind. Within ten minutes of my returning to the house with the drugs, things would go quickly down hill.

Going directly to the back bedroom, I would quickly begin to do three things at once. Placing all the drugs on the bed, I began to prepare the packages. I poured the cocaine on a mirror. There was one person waiting for an ounce of marijuana, and Pete was waiting for the tester. I prepared both of these, gave Denna the package to sell, and Pete the tester. He went into the bathroom to get off, taking drugs intravenously. Once I went back to work breaking down the drugs, I heard the voice of "Something" speak again.

He said, "The police are in the house."

There was no doubt in my mind what was happening in the house. I had given Denna a code to use if anything ever went wrong, but she didn't say a word. Not that this would have helped. Scraping the cocaine from the mirror, I hurriedly put the drug back into the zip-lock bag. I put the marijuana into a shopping bag. There was no way to hide two pounds of marijuana. I quickly moved to stand behind the door. Standing behind the door, I placed the zip-lock bag of cocaine inside my clothes.

And He shall hide
me in times of
trouble.

GOD'S GRACE

Now I have found grace in thy sight

While I was standing behind the door, the policeman knocked on the bedroom door and identified himself. Before the door could be opened, I needed to move from behind it. He allowed me time to move. When he entered the room, he instructed me to go into the living room to sit down with the other people in the house. Pete was caught in the bathroom with his syringe. Although I remember three of the officer's names that raided the house clearly, I won't identify them. The first reason being, one agreed to let me go to the bathroom. He didn't know it, but this gave me a chance to secure the cocaine more completely. The second reason being that by the time the marijuana was weighed and the charges made, several ounces of the drug were missing. Stranger yet, the person who had just bought the ounce of marijuana was allowed to leave the house immediately. Denna's mother, father, and boyfriend were also in the house. Her parents would eventually be allowed to leave.

The detectives had failed to produce a search warrant; therefore, I began to request that one be produced. They told me that this was not my house. I was hoping Denna would follow-up on this question, but she didn't. No warrant was ever produced. The detectives brought the shopping bag of marijuana out of the bedroom, and began to discuss who would be charged. They explained to Denna that since this was her house, she was definitely being charged. They asked her if she wanted to make any statement at this time. She made none. Waiting, I hoped that she would at least say let everybody else go. We could help her more if we were free. She remained silent. This was dumbfounding to me, since the possession of cocaine was a more severe charge. The detectives decided to arrest the four people remaining in the house. As we were escorted from the house, the neighbors were outside watching.

When we arrived at police headquarters for questioning, they began to process the papers. This was downtown on 1st Avenue, not in the actual jail. I asked if they were typing the request for the search warrant. There was no answer. There was a bulletin board in the room, and on that board was the name of the person who I was purchasing drugs from. We pretended that we didn't notice. From this room we were taken to the jail for further processing. Now, "Something" was still watching over me because when we arrived at the jail, everybody was strip searched, with the exception of me.

The cocaine was still on me, and I was scared that they would find the cocaine. If they had told me they were going to search me, I probably would have passed out from fear. We were taken to our cells. The men were housed in separate part of the jail. Denna and I were placed in the same cell on the third floor.

I had successfully gotten the drugs into the jail. However, I wasn't going to get caught with them or risk getting caught taking them back out. I didn't want to waste that much money either by flushing the drugs. There were approximately twenty other people in this cell, and between the two of us we knew most of them. However, only a few of these people would merit being included in the party that took place in the cell.

Comet and Baby Powder were sprinkled everywhere to kill the smell. Some people smoked the cocaine that I gave them in cigarettes. I swapped someone some Bugle tobacco and rolling papers, for some cocaine. I used this to come as close as I could to lacing a joint. We were able to judge when the guards would make their rounds in the cells. Also, usually there was only one guard assigned to the floor, if she had to leave the floor for any reason, the floor would be left unattended. This worked in our favor. We were trying to get rid of the cocaine so fast that we were making ourselves sick. One of us would be over the toilet puking, while the other one was bent over the sink doing the same.

With the cocaine gone I needed a plan to get us out of this mess. Getting out on bond had never been a problem for me before, but this time my bondsman was taking his time. Although, I had the money for the bond, he made me wait to be released. When he picked me up, he told me that he was getting tired of me doing stupid stuff, and had decided that I needed to sit there for a minute to think about what I was doing. He said he was also ticked off at me for asking him to get three additional people out of jail, without collateral. However, I wasn't worried about that, there was a bigger problem that I was worried about. Denna and I were both on probation. My probation officer had warned me that if I were ever arrested for drugs, he would recommend violating my probation. Sitting in the cell, I began to prepare one plan for Denna and one for me.

Immediately upon my release, I would begin working my plan, careful to follow every detail. The first step was to get Denna out before her probation officer found out about the arrests for Possession of Narcotics. She was on probation for the same type of offense. The night that I got out, I was about twenty dollars short of the money for Denna's bail. I went to her family for help but they wouldn't even help me with this small amount of money to secure her freedom. I was able to get her out the next day. I was able to move forward with my plan to ensure my probation officer wasn't going to lock me up. I needed to be the first person to tell him about my arrest. When I went to see him, I took with me a stack of letters from people in the community, and some professional agencies about how I had helped them. The letters were true. My plan came off better than I anticipated and resulted in my being allowed to stay out on bail until the he received the police report. He would make a final decision after reviewing this report.

Denna however, decided not to follow the plan I had given her. She had a probation officer that was a young Black man and he was new to the profession. Realizing that these should work in her favor, I told her to wear a provocative dress, and to go in begging. I told her to tell him that she would do anything to stay free, but to be careful not to proposition him. She decided not to talk to her probation officer. Once he found out about the charges, he issued a warrant for her arrest. It was only then that she wanted my help.

She called me and said, "My probation officer has issued a warrant for my arrest. What should I do now?"

I asked her why hadn't she gone to see him.

She said, "I didn't have time."

I knew that once the warrant had been issued, this had to be served, and she had to be arrested. There was nothing that I could do to stop the process.

The next day when she went to see the probation officer, he locked the door and called the police to pick her up. Her brother called me to tell me what had happened to her.

He stated, "Denna asked them what they were going to do about you. The probation officer explained to her that you weren't on his caseload and he didn't have anything to do with you."

I couldn't understand why she was asking about me, but this troubled me and was a dangerous warning sign. She knew that I had already reported to my probation officer what had happened.

After the police report came back and my probation officer received the report, he called me and told me that I would need to turn myself in to the Sheriff's Department at the Government Center. My probation hearing was scheduled for that Friday. I relayed this information to my attorney, and arrangements were made for me to turn myself in at 3:00 p.m., accompanied by my attorney.

When my lawyer and I arrived at the Sheriff's Department, the sheriff deputies searched, but they didn't have a warrant for my arrest. My attorney called my probation officer and he said he was bringing the warrant. As the Sheriff's Department was directly across from the District Attorney's Office, my attorney suggested that we go and ask the DA if he would be willing to let me remain free until the day of the probation hearing. This hearing would be necessary to determine if I had violated my probation. The District Attorney agreed to see us, and to my shock seemed to consider the request. When my probation officer arrived the DA asked for his recommendation.

"I don't have one. I told her that if she ever had a problem with drugs, I would recommend that she be locked up."

The DA requested to see my probation officer in private. Speechless, within myself I prayed and held my breath at the same time. When they returned, they told me something that I could believe. I was still free. The probation hearing was scheduled for the end of the week. I could remain free until the hearing.

That Friday, a probation hearing was held to determine my immediate fate. At my hearing, the detectives testified that the apartment was under surveillance for several weeks. They stated that they had never seen me at the apartment before. One of these statements had to be a lie, since I had been there every day for months. However, this worked in my favor. I wasn't about to correct them. My probation officer also reluctantly testified at this hearing. He tried to avoid making a statement, but the judge insisted that he make a recommendation.

"You have had more contact with her than anybody else. What do you know about her?"

With no choice left, he said, "She's paid her fees on time each month. She reports when she is scheduled. Sometimes, her children come to the office with her. The children are clean and well behaved. It appears that she takes good care of them."

No one else was aloud to testify. Denna's mother was angry she wanted to testify to make sure they locked me up with her daughter. This was in spite of the fact that I did lots of things to help her and her daughter. She kept waving her hand for the judge to recognize her but he never did. Her father however said if they asked him any questions, he was going to tell the truth.

At the end of the hearing, I was placed on intensive probation. This meant that I now had a 10:00 p.m. curfew. Several times a week two armed officers would verify that I complying with these conditions. This was embarrassing, because the neighbors observed them coming to my house, but the only other option was even more embarrassing. Additionally, I was given community service hours to complete. These hours were completed in one week. I wanted to get this out of the way. I was also required to report to the probation office several times a month. These requirements were a small price to pay for my freedom. Additionally, I was given a new probation officer. Mr. Green was very nice and went to bat for me, trying to ensure that I remained free. Believing that the intensive probation and community service was sufficient punishment for the crime, he began conferring with the judge, requesting that this serve as my sentence. After a couple of months, he was going to place me back on regular probation, but decided he needed to wait until a final decision was made in my case. His negotiations with the judge weren't going the way he expected. He didn't want anyone to think he had been too easy on me.

Charlotte Russell
AKA
Charlotte Johnson

PRAY WITHOUT CEASING

*And shall not God avenge His own elect, which cry day and night unto Him,
though He bear long with them?*

Immediately, God had my undivided attention. He was no longer
"Something." Now, He was "God." This time, I was really scared that I
might have to go to prison. The thought of going to prison wasn't appealing
to me. Actually, I found the thought repulsive. My mother was very patient
with me, regardless of my consistent failures. She never washed my face in
my mistakes. This wasn't the time for me to be hanging out in the streets
and I had no desire to be in the streets. Everybody was praying for me.
People came to my house to pray for me, and I went to other houses for
prayer. They weren't just praying. They were expecting answers to the
prayers. God was answering the prayers. There was one problem, the
answer. Over and over the answer came back, "When you go to court, tell
the truth." This wasn't exactly what I wanted to hear them say.

> *Likewise the Spirit also helpeth our infirmities: for we know not
> what we should pray for as we ought: but the Spirit itself maketh
> intercession for us with groanings that cannot be uttered. And he
> that searcheth the hearts knoweth what is the mind of the Spirit,
> because he maketh intercession for the according to the will of God.
> And we know that all things work together for good to them that love
> God, to them who are the called according to his purpose.*

Romans 8:26-28

During this time, I received the Baptism of the Holy Ghost and
joined a prayer band. All of the scriptures that I had ever learned came
flooding back to my memory. I was able to rightly divide the "Word of
Truth." I gave up smoking marijuana and drinking champagne. All my time
was spent reading the Word, in prayer meetings, Bible study, and going to
church.

Continuously, there was a search for a Word from the Lord on my
situation. The answers that I was getting weren't specific enough to ease my
troubled and worried mind. It didn't make sense to me that I should tell the
truth. The truth was that I was guilty. What I wanted was a miracle. I wanted
to be told that I wouldn't have to go prison. Trying to rationalize what I was
being told, I informed my lawyer that no matter what happened I wouldn't
be able to testify. This wasn't consistent with what I had been told, but this
was as close as my fear would let me come to the truth. In my mind, as long

as I didn't lie, I was telling the truth. There was no understanding that God was giving me instructions to voluntarily tell what had happened in the house that day.

Trying to reconcile my salvation with my living arrangements, I began witnessing to Buck. He promised that when he came home things would be different, and he would give up drugs. He was now due to come home within weeks. My divorce had been final for several months. I knew we wouldn't be able to continue living together without us being married, if I was to maintain my salvation. Once he was released, he didn't follow through on any of his promises. He immediately began the same habits that led to his arrest. The first day that he was out, he got high off heroin. Within the week, he was stealing again. Desperate to correct the problem, I began to use The Word to condemn his behavior. For this God convicted me, immediately.

One Sunday after being particularly hard on Buck, God revealed to me the transgression of my ways. Buck had promised me that if I went to bed that night, without continuously nagging him that he would go to church with me the next day. He wanted to be left him alone to finish getting high, without me blowing (ruining) the high. I left him alone, but the next morning he didn't follow through on his promise. Angrily, I began quoting scriptures to him. He gave no indication that he heard one word; therefore, I gave him additional scriptures. He never gave any response. We were taking communion that Sunday at church. The pastor instructed us to search ourselves to see if we were worthy to partake of the supper. A voice whispered to me.

"You're not worthy. What you just did caused a deep hurt."

Buck had shown no signs that he ever heard a word that was said to him. God gently reminded me that it is with kindness and love that He draws men to Him. My intentions were good; they were taken directly from the Word. They hadn't been taken out of context. However, I had carefully chosen each scripture to force Buck to see his wretchedness. Each time he didn't respond a firmer scripture pronouncing judgment was quoted. My words had been sharp, and they had pierced Buck to the bone.

Back to what happened when Buck first came home. The day after he was released we went to the parole office. There was a requirement that upon your release from prison in the state of Georgia on parole that you report to your parole officer within 24-hours. Buck informed the parole officer that we lived together before he was locked up, and we were planning to be married. The officer agreed that he could move back in the house with me. That was until he read through Buck's record and realized who his codefendant was. Buck had to return to the parole office the next day. Again, I was with him. When we entered his office together, he responded angrily.

"I should have locked you up yesterday when you came in here with her."

He would be making home visits to assure Buck was at his mother's house at night. This began a struggle for us to be at our house by 10:00 p.m. and at his mother's house by midnight. The problem was that sometimes my probation officers didn't come until almost midnight. Some nights it would be so late that I mistakenly assumed that they weren't coming. One night, we passed by them riding down the street headed to my house, as we were leaving. Buck had to turn the car around, rushing back to the apartment complex. While I was hurriedly entering the apartment through the back door, they were knocking at the front door. Luckily, they didn't know my car.

During the time that Denna was in jail she had become resentful of my being free. Once she had written me a letter telling me that if I didn't get her lawyer, she was going to tell that it was my dope. This told me enough about her intentions. We both knew the mail at the jail was subject to being screened, jailhouse lawyers (inmates) were influencing this process. Denna was only out on bond a couple of days before being locked up for the probation violation, and I had requested the $400 that I paid in bound fees be returned. The bondsman told me that he would think about this.

Denna had been in jail for several months and had continued to send me messages about what she planned to do: ensure that I went to prison. Denna's time remaining on probation expired, and she was again eligible to make bond. Members of her family contacted the bonding company about getting her out on bond. There was a major problem; I was still the person responsible for assuring that she showed up for court. I didn't know this person that was trying to send me to jail, and I wasn't able to guarantee anything about her. I never would have gotten busted in the first place, if she hadn't begged me to get that last package to help her out. I wanted the money that I had paid for her bond fee returned to me. Finally, someone else agreed to sign her bond, and give me my money back.

Do not lie in wait like an outlaw at the home of the godly. And don't raid the house where the godly live. They may trip seven times, but each time they will rise again. But one calamity is enough to lay the wicked low. Proverbs 24:15-16

As the time for my case to be brought to court drew closer, it became increasingly obvious that there would be no plea bargain. Denna wanted to be sure that I served some time in jail. The court system decided that we would be tried together. There would be one plea bargain or one trial. Our other codefendants would be tried separately. My probation officer was pushing for me to continue on probation as my sentence. The day of our trial, she was offered a one-year sentence, with credit being given for the time that she had already served in jail. Denna would also be eligible for consideration of parole. She wanted to know if I would have to serve any time in jail. Under the deal that was being offered, I would remain on Intensive Probation. She refused the plea bargain, and we went to trial, something that you shouldn't do when you are guilty.

Weighing heavily on my mind was, "Tell the truth." Again I reminded my attorney that I wouldn't be able to testify. As the trial progressed, each witness lied to suit his or her own purposes. Pete had cut a deal in exchange for the charges being dropped against him. He told everything on the witness stand. This included the process of injecting drugs intravenously. However, he conveniently forgot that he had requested the drugs from me. The other person that was arrested in the house refused to testify, and the charges were later dropped against him. My lawyer told me that I would have to testify since all blame was being placed firmly on me.

The thought of taking the stand was horrifying to me and this was extremely obvious. While on the witness stand, I was so nervous that I began to pop chewing gum and stutter profusely. In my mind was ringing, "Tell the truth." How could I tell the truth? The judge instructed me to take the chewing gum out of my mouth. I fumbled miserably through the testimony. When I returned to sit next to my lawyer at the defense table, he leaned over and told me that I was the worst liar that he had ever seen. He told me that I had basically sealed my own fate. I asked him what was the maximum sentence that I could receive for possession of cocaine and possession of marijuana. Although, the detectives had testified that the amount of cocaine found on the mirror was to small to measure, the possession of cocaine was the more serious of the two charges. He told me that I didn't want to know the maximum sentence. My Aunt Bobbie had been in the courtroom with me. She encouraged me to leave town to avoid going to prison. I didn't want to run for the rest of my life. I decided that I would tough this out, although, the thought of going to prison was repulsive to me.

And of whom hast thou been afraid or feared, that thou hast lied, and hast not remembered me, nor laid it to thy heart? have not I held my peace even of old, and thou feareth me not? Isaiah 57:11

During the court recess, Buck and I were married. Resigned that I was going to prison, I didn't want to go broke. I needed enough money to last until I was released. By my calculations, under the Georgia Parole Guidelines, I would only serve 4-5 months. I needed at least five hundred dollars. We went stealing, and I got the funds that I needed. Later, I got a bottle of champagne and a bag of marijuana. That night I went to bed, leaving Buck up getting high. The day's events had exhausted me. The next morning, I grabbed another bottle of champagne, a champagne glass, and a couple of joints, and we headed to court for my sentence.

To ensure that there were two convictions, the judge gave a very detailed description of the meaning of possession, because all of the testimony had been conflicting.

He said, "My car keys are in my pocket, therefore, they are in my actual possession. My car is downstairs in the garage, therefore, it's in my inactual possession."

After deliberating for a while, the jury returned to ask the judge to explain the meaning of possession again. The next time that the jury returned, they had reached a guilty verdict.

According to them, "We find them guilty of inactual possession."

This meant that the drugs were found in the house, even if we didn't realize they were there, we had access to them. They couldn't be sure who knew the drugs were there, but according to the judge's definition, if the drugs weren't in our actual possession, they would have been in our inactual possession.

I think the judge unfairly influenced the jury, but during the sentencing, he was the first person to "Tell the truth." He described me as a wholesaler and Denna as a retailer. He said the disagreement was because she hadn't paid me for the drugs. This summed things up, fairly accurately. He gave me a fifteen-year sentence for the possession of Cocaine, and ten years for the Possession of Marijuana. Both sentences would run concurrent. He had given me the maximum sentence for the charge. If only I had "Told the truth." Denna was given ten years for each count of possession. This would also run concurrent. The next day an article would appear in the newspaper about the trial, causing my mother additional embarrassment.

While we were being escorted from the courtroom by the sheriffs, I turned to Denna.

"We started out in this together, now we are going to prison together. Would you like a hug?"

She nodded and I reached over to hug her. When we got to the jail we requested that we be assigned to the same cell. The news of these sentences beat us to the jail. The rumor was that I had received twenty-five years. I took my Bible to my room and placed it up under my pillow. This position was chosen to keep the Word literally near my head. This gave me the assurance that I wouldn't lose my mind under the weight of the sentence. Jailhouse lawyers (inmates) began to define my future. According to their expertise, I would spend at least five to seven years in prison before being released on parole. My confession was unwavering, I would be locked up for four to five months. I needed to believe this, to keep my sanity. I spent most of my time reading scriptures in the Book of Psalm. These scriptures assured me that because so many people were rejoicing at my downfall, God was going to deliver me.

Let not them that are mine enemies wrongfully rejoice over me: neither let them wink with the eye that hate me without a cause. Psalm 35:19

Immediately, I began writing letters to the Sentence Review Panel of Georgia requesting that they review my sentence, because this was excessive. I collected articles from newspapers that were written about the sentence that other people charged with Possession received. These were also sent to the panel with a request that they compare the sentence that I receive with those imposed in these cases. There were no sentences even remotely close to mine. At this time, I had a longer sentence than anyone that I knew of in the jail, with the exception of Carlton Gary (someone who is an **alleged** serial killer).

THE HONEYMOON

By night I sought him whom my soul loveth:
I sought him, but I found him not.

This was turning out to be some kind of honeymoon. The suite wasn't exactly the best in the house, bunk with whomever you can until you can get a private suite. There was room service, but no choices from the menu. There was no private Jacuzzi, but a public shower without doors, with windows that faced the main hall. Anyone walking by from two sides could observe you bathing. This was a point of contention for me, because people wanted to see my scars. There was no way that I was going to accommodate this desire. Rather than endure the humiliation, I took birdbaths in my room. There was no plush carpet but concrete floor. There was no down filled bed and satin sheets, but a metal bed with a thin plastic mattress. There were midnight chats, as the other inmates discussed how crazy I was to keep saying that I would be going home in a few months.

Before the end of the month, my new husband would join me for the honeymoon, however, not by coming to share my suite. There was a separate suite reserved for him, with his name on it. He was assigned to the fifth floor, and I was housed on the third floor. He began to make arrangements to secure the room directly above mine. You see the Muscogee County Jail has a rather unique communicating system. Somehow the toilets are connected between the floors. If you pumped the water in the toilet out and disinfected the toilet with Comet, newspaper could be used to make a kind of horn. The horn extended from the toilet allowing your voice to travel through the newspaper and through the pipes. Thus you were able to talk between floors. This was how we spent our honeymoon, bent over the toilet talking to each other.

Buck had ignored all of my warnings to stop stealing. There was one specific store that I had repeatedly warned him not to go back into. This is where he was caught. I had dreamed that he would be caught soon in this store. Therefore, his arrest wasn't really a surprise to me. However, his being locked up made me really angry with him. Now, I didn't know when I would see him again. Also, I had stood by him while he was incarcerated; he had a responsibility to the same for me. Him standing by me was actually a fantasy that I had. I knew that drugs were his first love. Buck was calm about the whole thing, almost relieved. My mind was torn now, the sooner I was sent off to prison, the sooner I would be able to make parole. But being sent off also meant that I wouldn't be able to talk to him or see him. There would be a couple of months before the next group of women prisoners would be sent to Hardwick, Georgia. At this time, the only women's prison in the state was located in Hardwick. This gave us some time to do limited bonding.

My mother would now have the sole responsibility of coming to see me, and providing for my needs while I was locked up. The next time she came to see me, I made my expectations clear. After assuring her again that I would be out in four to five months, (actually I was assuring myself) I told her I wanted her to come see me on Saturdays and Sundays. I also wanted a letter from her at least once a week. When I got to the prison, there would be additional things that I wanted from her. I wanted to be able to call home at least once a week, and I wanted a package every month. As if appeasing a spoiled brat, my mother agreed to all of this. Fateful as usual, she held true to her word. Additionally, my mother was left with the responsibility of caring for my children.

In order for her to effectively care for my children, I needed to give her temporary custody of my children. Although this was temporary, this was the hardest part of being locked up. This seemed almost final in my mind. I prided myself on taking good care of my children. Even during the times when I wasn't hustling and my finances were tight, I found money to take them shopping regularly. They spent a lot of time with Mama because I didn't want them exposed to the streets, but I was always able to pick them up. The day my lawyer brought the papers to the jail for me to sign was one of the hardest days that I spent in jail. When my lawyer arrived, I was called outside of the cell to meet with him in a private room. As I cried, he assured me that all Mama had to do was give me my children back when I came home. Still I was giving up my parental rights, "temporally" didn't make this easier.

Early one morning, the names were called of the people who were leaving in fifteen minutes for Hardwick. My name was one of about twelve names called. Hurriedly, I tried to wake Buck up so that I could say goodbye, while at the same time throwing my limited belongings into a pillowcase. About 6:30 a.m., we were shipped off to Hardwick. We were being shipped off before the holidays. This was the first time that I had been outdoors in more than two months. Outside never looked so good.

Immediately upon our arrival at the prison, we were fingerprinted, and photographed again. We were provided wardrobes for our stay that consisted of three pairs of khaki-colored pants with matching short sleeve tops. We were assigned rooms in a section of the prison referred to as Diagnostics. These buildings were separated from the main prison population by a locked fence. The inmates who were in isolation or on Death Row were also housed in this area of the prison. Whenever new prisoners arrived, the other prisoners wanted to get a look at them, mostly to see if there was anyone that they knew coming in. They were also anxious to get word from home. Shortly after we arrived, the word spread about the length of my sentence. Strangers were coming up to me asking me if it was true that I had twenty-five years. They also wanted to know what made me think I was only going to serve only four to five months. My confession was the same, although I knew within my heart that the delay in being shipped out from the jail might delay my parole.

The prison at Hardwick was set up like a college dormitory for women. With the exception of the barbed wire that surrounded the prison, and the guards, there were no indications that this was a prison. Prisoners were allowed to wear their own shoes and accessories. There was also a beauty salon. If you could get the chemicals for you hair sent to you from home, you could keep your hair styled in elaborate styles. Occasionally, you would see an inmate who was in solitary confinement. White jumpsuits and handcuffs on their hands identified them. Sometimes there were also shackles on their feet that served as further identification. They were prisoners within prison. At first glance this appeared to be a coed prison. It took me a few minutes to realize that some of the men in khaki-colored uniforms were actually women. The most shocking thing of all was discovering that some of the myths about prison weren't true. One myth was immediately put to rest, the one about the way people in prison were raped. While we were in diagnostics, before we ever made it to general population, my roommate received several letters from people saying, "I've never had a relationship with a woman, but I'm willing to learn. Will you teach me?"

There were no bars on the windows and most of the dorms were actually nice on the outside. Now as for the food, there were a lot of soybean products served. We were served fried chicken and barbecue pork chops once a month. These were the only decent meals. The food was prepared off site at a kitchen that prepared food for several prisons in the area. Some of the prisoners were assigned to work in this kitchen. If you had a good relationship with one of these women, you could get extra snacks. They often stole food from the kitchen, and brought this back to be sold in the dorm. A favorite meal was grilled cheese sandwiches. These were prepared by wrapping a cheese sandwich in notebook paper. The sandwich was toasted by sitting the steam iron on the sandwich. There was one day a week that we were allotted to purchase items from the store. Store is an over statement, because most of the items consisted of crackers, cookies, chips, and limited personal hygiene items. We were allowed to spend a maximum of $25 dollars a week. Make no mistake about it; we never forgot that we were in prison.

Each inmate was assigned a counselor. This was the person that I wanted to talk to. When I told her that by my calculations I would only serve four to five months, she stated that she didn't know of anybody with my charges having a sentence even close to mine. I assured her that I would only be there a few months. As things would go, the parole board was running slow in sending out parole decisions. Denna got her decision back first. She would have to serve a total of seventeen months. They gave her credit for the time that she had already served. When I received my guideline back the board had deviated from the grid recommendations of four to five months, and added six months to the time that I was required to serve in prison. By this time, I had already served six months. I would be going home in four to five months.

Now, the jailhouse lawyers changed their messages. There were two new messages. The first one, "I knew you wouldn't be here long." That's not what they told me. The second message was even more ridiculous, "Don't let them trick you like that. They know that you will be back." There were people who had been shipped to Hardwick with me that had one-year sentences. I would be going home before every person that had rejoiced over my predicament. Contrary to popular opinions and statistics, I wouldn't be going back to prison. Once was enough for me.

Buck had been assigned to Jack T. Rutledge State Prison in Columbus. We had received special permission to write and were communicating regularly. The band from Jack Rutledge was coming to perform at the prison where I was incarcerated in Hardwick. We learned that we might be able to obtain special permission for Buck to travel with the band for a special visit with me. This would require approval from the warden at both prisons. This worked out and we were able to have a visit that lasted several hours. This was the highlight of my prison stay. Of course, the visit was monitored closely.

Look thou upon me, and be merciful unto me, as thou usest to do unto those that love thy name. Order my steps in thy word: and let not iniquity have dominion over me. Deliver me from the oppression of man: so that I will keep thy precepts. Make thy face to shine upon thy servant; and teach me thy statutes. Psalms 119:132-135

After being incarcerated for eleven months, I was finally released. There was one thing that I wanted to eat, fried chicken. My friend Esther drove down to pick me up. My mother and children came with her. Mama had gotten up early that morning to cook the chicken, and she had made homemade biscuits. This was the first thing that I wanted when I got in the car. I had been craving fried chicken for almost a year. When we got back to Columbus, they dropped me off at Jack Rutledge to see Buck. This was a surprise visit for him. This would begin my weekly visits to the prison to see him. I had survived my own prison ordeal.

Then I said I would not make mention of Him, nor speak anymore in His name. But His word was in my heart as a burning fire shut up in my bones, and I was weary with forbearing, and could not stay. Jeremiah 20:9

While I was locked up, I had faithfully read my Bible. I also attended regular Bible studies and church services in the prison chapel. I had even spoken a couple of times during the services. Although, I wasn't scheduled to speak, this was something that I took upon myself. The chaplain at the prison lacked the ability to encourage rehabilitation in the prisoners. The first time that I attended one of the services, she made a very discouraging statement.

"I know that some of you have been praying for God to get you out of here. By now, you should have realized that isn't going to happen."

I didn't consider this sound doctrine. Later, I would give my own discourse on the power of God. No matter how long it would take, whenever we left the prison, this would be because God allowed it.

Lord how they are increased that trouble me! Many are they that rise up against me. Many are they that wish to say of my soul, There is no help for him in God. But thou, O Lord, art a shield for me; my glory, and the lifter up of mine head. I cried unto the Lord with my voice, and he heard me out of his holy hill. I laid me down to slept; I awakened for the Lord sustained me. I will not be afraid of ten thousands people, that have set themselves against me round about. Psalm 3:1-6

My intention upon my release was to get actively involved in a good church. I went to church a couple of times after I got out, but not consistently. There was still a bad taste in my mouth from my previous experiences. Additionally, Earline had told me that one Sunday, while

Mama was visiting me at the jail, the pastor had embarrassed her by openly rebuking Herman.

The pastor stopped preaching and told Earline, "If you can't control him, you need to take him out."

Earline took Herman and left the church. Mama arrived as my children were heading home. My children were already going through enough. They didn't need this additional embarrassment. Although I was no longer angry about this, the memory was still in the back of my mind. Procrastination and complacency would make it easy for me to loose sight of my promises to God. It seemed that the only thing that I had really made up my mind about was that I didn't want to sell drugs again. My prison sentence, if I was caught, was already defined, fourteen years and one month. This sentence was long enough to make any sane person think twice about committing another crime.

TALLY-HO

Let favor be shewed to the wicked, yet he will not learn righteousness:
in the land of uprightness will he deal unjustly,
and will not behold the majesty of the Lord.

Now that my feet were back on the ground, it would only take me a few days to get another car. This was a necessity for me to function comfortably. I had a grand total of $300 to get the car. My uncle and one of our friends would take me riding to look for the car. We found something that would suit my needs temporarily. This was all that I wanted, something to hold me until I got on my feet. It would be necessary to put oil in the car every day, but at least I was riding. If I had transportation I could maneuver anything else. Now, I could concentrate on moving out on my own. Before the month was out, I had rented a trailer and moved out.

Herman was attending a daycare center downtown. It was necessary for me to drive him to school each morning. One morning when I was taking Herman to school, we stopped by Ma'Dear's house. Ma'Dear always had something to give the children whenever they came by her house. Herman had a bad habit of jumping out the car wherever it stopped. On this morning, I caught him before he was able to get out of the car. After we left Ma'Dear's house we drove towards the Thirteenth Street Bridge. Below this bridge were train tracks. There was only a low wall (maybe less than two feet high) that served as the only barrier along the bridge to prevent you from falling off the bridge and down onto the train track. This wasn't much of a barrier. If you staggered too close to the edge, you could easily fall off the bridge. The traffic was always heavy on weekdays around this time of the morning. When I turned left onto the bridge, the car door swung open on Herman's side of the car. Herman, now four years old, was holding onto the door and bouncing up and down. There were cars coming behind me. Afraid to stop to fast because I feared that his grip would be broken or that someone would hit me from behind, I eased the car to a stop. He had been holding the inside door handle, since we left Ma'Dear's house. Calmly, he climbed back into the car. When we got to the school, I checked him carefully to be sure he wasn't hurt. He never cried and made only one statement.

"My shoestrings broke."

He was wearing new tennis shoes. The torn shoestrings were the only sign of this ordeal. When I told Mama what had happen to him, she said during the night she had a strong urge to pray.

"I started to pray laying in the bed, but I could tell that God wanted me to get on my knees. I obeyed and got down on my knees and began to pray. I'm glad that I obeyed."

Herman never stopped jumping out of the car. This was just one of his many adventures.

Later, I would assist one of my friends, Pat, in purchasing a trailer in the same trailer park. This led to a part time job for me selling trailers, not that I was looking for a job. The man who owned the lot asked me to help him out. He was impressed by the way Pat trusted my judgment, considering the differences in our ages. Pat was at least ten years older than I was. This would open the door for me to purchase my own trailer. The trailer that I was living in was owned by a slumlord. Every time it rained, the roof leaked in several parts of the house, particularly my bedroom. Each time the roof leaked, I would ask the landlord to repair the roof, and this would be patched. The next time it rained, the cycle repeated itself.

My furniture was constantly sitting in wet carpet. Afraid that I was going to loose all of my furniture, I explained my situation to one of the men that I was selling mobile homes for. I asked if he had anything that I could rent, but he preferred to sale me a trailer. My credit wasn't sufficient to get the trailer financed in my name. He told me if I could come up with a small down payment, he would finance the trailer himself. He gave me a good interest rate, and a good price. By the end of the day, I was moving into my own trailer. It was snowing, but this wasn't going to stop me from getting out of that dump. We managed to get everything moved shortly before the electric power was knocked out from the snowstorm.

My mother and I had talked for several years about opening a restaurant. However, we weren't doing anything to move towards this direction. After one of the men at the mobile home lot cheated me out a commission, I had quit working at the trailer park. Pat worked at a soul-food restaurant downtown. Mr. Stone owned the restaurant. He also owned another restaurant, the Tally-Ho. One day, Pat called me and said Mr. Stone wanted to know if I was interested in the Tally-Ho. I responded that I really wasn't interested in working.

She responded, "I don't think he wants you to work for him. Just come talk to him."

I didn't really know Mr. Stone and the only thing that he knew about me was that Pat respected my opinions.

Curious, I went to talk to Mr. Stone. The conversation lasted all of five minutes.

He said simply, "Do you think you could handle the Tall-Ho."

I responded just as simply, "Yes sir."

He told me to make a list of all the items that I would need to open the restaurant, and asked me to come back the next day. Still unsure what he had in mind, I showed up the next day with my list. He took me to the grocery store and purchased everything that I had on my list and gave me the keys to the restaurant. His only instructions were for me to come see him after I had completed my first week.

We opened the restaurant without even a dollar to go in the cash register. The menu consisted of a large variety of soul food, chitterlings, ribs, pig feet, pig ears, black-eyed peas, collard greens, macaroni and cheese, and homemade sweet potato pies, etc. We served breakfast and lunch. My mother would assist with cooking before she went to work each morning. On her lunch hour, and again when she finished her regular job with the Housing Authority, she would return to help me with cooking and serving the food.

That first Saturday evening after we closed, I went to see Mr. Stone. He wanted to know if I had purchased the additional supplies that I would need for the following week and paid my help. Only after these items were taken care of, he wanted 25% of what remained. I didn't tell him that during the week someone (someone close to my heart) working for me had also stolen all of my money from the cash register. Mr. Stone was an accountant and included in the 25% that he received would be the cost of him completing my taxes for the business. He further told me that when I was comfortable with the restaurant, I could just give him $125 a month for the use of the equipment and assume responsibility for the other expenses. The other expenses were less than $200 a month. A month later, I would take over the restaurant completely.

The Tally-Ho was full of rats that looked more like cats. They had lived there for years and threatened to put me out. We were constantly setting rat traps. If I had known about these residents, I never would have agreed to run the restaurant. Mama would go into the building first each morning, making sure that it was safe for me to enter. If I heard a trap spring and I was in the restaurant by myself, I would run outside. There I waited, outside of the restaurant mortified. Eventually, one of the regular customers, knowing about the problem in the area, would come to my rescue. They would go take care of the problem for me, while I waited outside for them to dispose of the rats (cats). One day a customer told me that she had seen a rat run across the counter. I came from behind the counter, went out the door, leaving her in the restaurant, and ran down the street. Sometimes, if I heard something, I would just stand outside and cry. There wasn't much that I was afraid of, but I was scared of rats and mice, especially ones that looked like cats.

Buck was really excited about the restaurant, but this excitement wouldn't be prolonged. He was getting close to being released from prison. I had kept my promise not to sell drugs again and I didn't want to go back down that road. Things were going well with my parole. The day he was released, my semi-normal life would be upset again. The first day he was out, I overheard someone offer him a package of crack.

I answered for him, "No, he's not going to back to that mess."

There was no way we were going to get involved with this lifestyle again, or so I thought. A few days later, when we returned home from the Tally-Ho, I turned around to tell him something, but he was gone. There were no signs of Buck outside. My heart fell prostrate. I knew where he had gone.

Determined to teach him a lesson, I drove the car around the street and hid it. Not wanting Pat to worry if he told her that I was missing, I went across the street and told her that I would be in the trailer. Since I had bought the trailer while Buck was in prison, he didn't know where the light switches were. The kids were at Mama's house. Turning out all the lights in the house, I laid in Herman's bed, and covered up to wait. When he returned, he began fumbling through the house looking for the light switches, to no avail.

He began calling out, "CJ, where are you?"

I laid still and remained silent. Frantically, he went back out the door. I knew he was headed to Pat's. Still, I didn't move. Within a few minutes he returned. This time when he returned, he was still screaming, but he was also feeling his way through every room in the house, and every inch of the rooms. Finally, he located my left foot. From there he found my face, but he was still scared.

"CJ, say something. Are you all right?"

Rudely, I responded, "Take your hands off me!"

He didn't tell me that he had picked up the package of crack. I don't know how long he thought that he would be able to maintain this secret.

Sundays were the only days that the Tally-Ho was closed. This was our day to go out to an upscale restaurant for dinner. This Sunday, he made a stop and left me in the car, as he went into a relative's house. This was unusual considering where he had stopped. When he returned, his face confirmed my worst fears. While he had been locked up, a lot of people that we knew had begun smoking crack. He didn't know who they were, but I knew quite a few of them. This was one of them. My decision was to put things on the table. He had given this person a package to sell. They had smoked it up. Knowing that he had made grave mistakes in issuing out the packages, I asked him for the names of everyone else that he had give a package. He gave me one other name.

"Go by to check on your money. Everything that you have issued out has gone up in smoke"

His next stop proved me right. This was another person who was now hooked on crack. In spite of these mistakes, my desire was not to become involved with moving the drugs. When asked about the quantity of drugs that he had picked up, he responded.

"A half a keyload."

A half-a-key is sixteen ounces. Wanting to be sure the drugs weren't stashed near my children or me, I asked where the drugs were. This was the most shocking and hurting revelation. An elderly relative was holding the drugs for him. This was more courage than I had, and I wasn't actually running short on fortitude.

People started coming by the Tally-Ho prepared to buy drugs. No matter what was said, they wouldn't believe that drugs weren't on the menu. The money started coming fast, and I decided that it would be necessary for me to get involved, managing the money. My concern was that the money would come up short and I would be held accountable for it too. Things started to get out of hand. Buck was ignoring all my warnings. He brushed this off as my usual nagging. I had learned a hard lesson about helping friends keep their drug business open. He was about to walk over into the same trap.

The more money that Buck made selling drugs the less he desired to work at the Tally-Ho. To compensate for this he began paying all the expenses of the Tally-Ho. He was constantly buying me things. Every Sunday, he took me to an upscale restaurant. When we left the restaurant, he took me shopping for anything that my heart desired. Rather than working, he would give Earline anything that she wanted to work in his place. Still, This didn't appease me and my complaining continued.

Earline was in the seventh grade at this time. Typical of most seventh graders, she became bored with working at the Tally Ho after school. She wanted to spend more time playing with her friends and participating on the cheerleading squad.

Buck walked into the Tally-Ho one day with some of his old "get high buddies." He told me that he was only with them because they were bringing me clothes. Staring him dead in his face, it was obvious that his lips were twisted and his moth was parched. I fell to the floor weeping.

Trying to reassure me, he said, "It was only one time."

His reassurance didn't work. We had been down this road before, and we both knew all the intersections, and the final destination.

One day, Buck left the Tally-Ho and he was gone for an extremely long time. He didn't call me, and this was peculiar. People were continuously coming by the Tally-Ho looking for him, but he was nowhere to be found. It was getting close to the time for the Tally-Ho to close and he still wasn't back. Finally, I called his niece and asked her to pick me up from work. Buck had some crack stashed outside the Tally-Ho. When she picked me up, the crack was taken with me. As we rode down the street, I threw the crack out the window.

Our time at home was suppose to be time when we left the stress of the streets behind. Few people had our home telephone number, and we didn't sell or keep drugs in the house. One night after we returned home, Buck's niece called and wanted a package. He told her that he was in for the night. Knowing that she wouldn't take no for an answer, we turned all the lights out in the trailer. I asked Buck if he had hid the crack that he brought home.

He responded by saying, "It's only crumbs. I don't feel like moving it. If she finds it, let her have it."

She had a car that you could hear a block away. As we were sitting quietly in the living room, we heard the sound of the ragged car coming. We eased to the kitchen window, and watched when she stopped directly in front of the trailer. She didn't come to the door, but instead searched around the front door, going almost immediately to the bag of cookie crumbs (small pieces of crack). We laughed when she got back in the car and drove off.

Buck had been out of drugs for a couple of weeks. David, a friend (what he thought was a friend) of Buck's had asked him to serve as the middleman to pick up cookies (one cookie is an ounce of crack) for him. Jay, the person selling the drugs, wouldn't deal directly with this man, David. Jay knew David but didn't trust him. After this exchange had gone a couple of times, Jay asked Buck if he wanted to hold a cookie until the next time David called. When we arrived home one night, David called. This ticked me off because he wasn't supposed to have our home telephone number. He was asking Buck a lot of questions over the telephone. Questions that he already had the answers to. He asked him if the cookie was whole or cut up. In the background, my protests kept cutting the conversation off. To no avail, I tried to get Buck not to meet him.

Shortly after Buck left the house to meet him, David called back to our home. Originally, Buck was suppose to meet him at his grocery store, David's Grocery. He wanted to change the meeting to a parking lot near a nightclub. He was trying to get me involved in the transaction. He was rudely instructed to leave me out of that mess. Within minutes of him hanging up the telephone, my mother-in-law called to tell me that the police were shooting at Buck in her back yard.

Obviously upset, she said, "You need to get here quick. The police are shooting at your husband out here."

Upon my arrival at her house, I pulled up behind David's truck, parked on the left-hand side of the street. Shocked to see David's truck, I forgot momentarily to look for Buck. I was dumb struck to see that David wasn't driving the truck. A man with handcuffs extending from the back left pocket of his pants was climbing into the driver's seat of the truck. The complete picture wasn't fully developed, but clearly, the man driving the truck was a detective. The tag number was recorded for future reference. On the right-hand side of the street was parked my brown Cavalier. Buck was nowhere in obvious sight. The front door of the car was open and a detective was getting into the front seat. I walked over to him.

"Excuse me. This is my car."

He responded sure of himself, "This car is being confiscated by the City of Columbus and the police department."

Just as sure, I responded, "Did you find drugs in MY CAR?"

I was sure Buck wouldn't have left the drugs in the car.

He shot back, "No! But the driver of this car has been arrested, and he was involved in a drug transaction."

Again, I wanted to know about the drugs, "Did you find any drugs?"

He answered without thinking; "We found a half an ounce of crack in the woods."

Looking around, I didn't see Buck. "Can you tell me what happened to the driver?"

Vaguely, he responded, "You can call the jail later."

Buck had been taken to the hospital, but this wouldn't be known until hours later. After the police left, I would get Buck's brother to drive me past David's house. His cream colored Toyota truck was parked back in his yard. Again, the tag number verified.

When I got back home, David called me, attempting to offer a pathetic explanation.

"Charlotte, where is Buck?"

Angrily I responded, "You tell me?"

Then he started with a lie that didn't even make sense to him.

"I tried to call back to tell him not to meet me. The police kidnapped me, and left me handcuffed in the woods. The detectives took my truck. When they came back, I didn't know what they did with it."

Silently, I listened to his explanation, knowing what he had done to my husband. Buck called after he was released from the hospital, and taken to jail. He told me that the police had pistol-whipped him. He wanted me to get him out of jail before his parole officer found out what had happened. This would need to be done quickly. The next day, $10,000 cash was spent to get him out.

When Buck was released from jail, there were stitches in the center of his head, and bruises covered most of his body. He told me how two officers held him pinned to the ground in the woods, while two others beat him. He further told me that during his time in the holding cell at the jail, he talked to a man who had gotten busted earlier in the evening. The man said that he had been busted with David, but he didn't know what happened to David. I did. David owed Buck some money, and Buck wanted me to go pick this up. However, he was afraid that my conduct wouldn't be rational. Reluctantly, the call was placed to David and he was informed that the money needed to get Buck out of jail. My uncle went with me to pick the money up from David's house. David was nervous and still trying to explain. With my eyes, I was trying burn a hole in him, so that the truth could run out the hole.

Buck gave me the man's name (Benny Thomas) that had been in the holding cell with him. The name is fictitious. I called the jail to find out when the man was scheduled to appear in Recorder's Court. Without explaining what had happened to Buck, I asked a lady that worked for me at the Tally-Ho to go to this man's hearing along with my daughter. My request was for them to sit at the front of the courtroom to be sure that they got all the details of the hearing. When they returned from court, they had the complete details, not only of this man's arrest but Buck's arrest as well.

They described everything, including the two telephone calls from the police station that were placed to my home. They discussed in great details the deal that they made with David. Additionally, they found out that the original location of the setup had to be changed because there was too much traffic near David's grocery store that night.

This is how Buck was busted. Benny met a man at club on Steam Mill Road. The man, who was an undercover detective, asked him if he knew where he could get some crack. The detective promised Benny a small piece of the $20 rock. Benny called David, who lived nearby. Benny wasn't allowed to go directly to David's house so they met at the store on the corner of Northstar Drive and St. Mary's Road, about five blocks away. When David arrived, they went in the store to make the transaction. The detectives were already in place on the outside of the store, and the money was marked. David and Benny were both arrested. The detectives offered both of them a deal in exchange for their freedom. If they could give them someone with a larger quantity of drugs, the charges against them would be dropped. When they arrived at the jail, David accepted the deal. He called Buck from the jail to make arrangements for the setup. Originally, they planned for the arrest to take place at David's store in East Wynnton. When the detectives got to the street where the store was located, a lot of people were walking around, and this was too dangerous to set up the operation. They asked David to call back to our house to change the location of the rendezvous. When Buck arrived at the store he didn't see David. He stopped at a telephone booth and called me. Buck was informed of the second telephone call from David. The second location was in a shopping center on Buena Vista Road, not far from Buck's mother's house. When Buck pulled up next to David's truck, the detective jumped out of David's truck. The detective grabbed the locked car door, as Buck sped off heading for familiar woods, behind his mother's house. The detectives were right behind him. Buck managed to throw the drugs into the woods before the detectives ran him down. Somehow, the ounce of crack was a half an ounce of crack when it reached the jail. Ironically, the officer that told me about the weight of the crack had also been involved in my drug arrest.

To avoid going back to jail, Buck left town for a while. His parole officer began looking for him. This included watching the Tally-Ho, and dropping in frequently. This probably helped to ruin business at the Tally-Ho. My parole officer was also making visits to the restaurant but not as frequently. The restaurant had been opened more than a year. The Tally-Ho was more work than we had imagined. The restaurant had taken control of our lives and we were all tired of this. Often when we left the Tally-Ho at the end of the day, I was scarcely able to make it to the car. I had also gotten accustomed to having quick and fast money again.

The finance company was able to get my car back from the police department, after a couple of months. When a drunk driver ran into the car, a few months later, it was decided, it was time to close the Tally-Ho. I wasn't seriously hurt in the accident, but this gave me the excuse that was needed to close the restaurant.

Charlotte R. Johnson
Is money the answer?
***Does money buy peace, happiness, love, salvation
or the love of Jesus Christ?***

PROTECTED BY HIS GRACE

And when I passed by thee, and saw thee polluted in thine own blood,
I said unto thee when thou wast in thy blood, Live; yea,
I said unto thee when thou wast in thy blood, Live.

While running the Tally-Ho, there were a lot of thieves coming in and out to sell their commodities. Buck bought me anything that I wanted in an effort to appease me for having to be implicated in this lifestyle. However, my protesting never stopped. Dee was one of my friends that were keeping my wardrobe outfitted. I'll refer to her as Dee. This isn't her name. She called me Queen. Dee had been hospitalized several times during this period, but had quickly recovered. Now that the Tall-Ho was closed, and she was out of the hospital, we would spend more time together. We were mostly shoplifting. Again, my role was picking out the clothes or pulling (distracting the sales person). There was another person that was with us occasionally, Betty. Dee almost gave away whatever she stole. She would sell everything at below bargain prices. There was nothing that anybody could do to persuade her to charge the normal street prices.

In the time of trouble he shall hide me in his pavilion: in the secret of his tabernacle shall he hide me; he shall set me up upon the rock.
Psalm 27:5

One day when I was taking Dee stealing, she got into a physical confrontation with her boyfriend, in Buck's car. We were driving through the East Wynnton area. Buck was still out of town in hiding. She wanted her boyfriend to stay behind, as we went on the mission. She was concerned that the way he was dressed would draw unneeded attention in the better stores. He wasn't opposed to staying behind, but he wanted her to get some money from me to get him a sack of heroin. She refused to ask me for the money and they started arguing. The argument escalated, forcing me to stop in the middle of the street. They began fighting in the back seat of the car. One of them broke a pint gin bottle during the fight. He began to beat her with the bottle. Then he pulled her in the street and told me to pull off. When I wouldn't do this, he walked off leaving her lying in the street. She crawled tediously back into the front seat of the car.

A lady that was standing nearby approached the car, after he walked off.

She said, "Wait Charlotte. Let me get a towel. She's bleeding."

This was when I noticed that Dee was bleeding. Her arm had been cut in several places. She was bleeding very freely, and the blood was spraying from her arm like a fountain. This was something that I had never witnessed before. The lady returned with a towel to wrap Dee's arm. In order to avoid to answering questions about what had happened, and charges being pressed against him, she didn't want to go to the hospital. The police were sure to be called if she went to the hospital. She asked me to take her home. When we got to her house, her mother wasn't home, and I was afraid that she would bleed to death if I left her there. Against her wishes, she was driven to the hospital.

When we got to the emergency room, because she was bleeding so heavy, the other patients said that she could be seen first. I filled out the admission papers for her. A nurse came out and placed something over the wound to limit the bleeding, until she could be taken to the back for the examination. Her mother called and the incident was explained to her. She arrived at the hospital a few minutes later. The police were indeed called, but Dee didn't tell them what happened, and I remained silent. Her clothes were soaked with blood. After she had been treated, and the doctor decided to release her, I got another outfit from the car for her to wear. She went home with her mother.

My children were with my mother, and needed to be picked up, before I went home. It was only then that my thought turned to AIDS. These thoughts hadn't crossed my mind before now. My only concern had been assuring that my friend wouldn't bleed to death. Once this was assured, the amount of blood in the car concerned me. From the Emergency Room, my mother called and asked to meet me at my car with a towel soaked in bleach. While in prison, we had been given AIDS education, but at that time I really didn't listen. This was a disease that happened to other people. The only thing that I remembered was that bleach and gloves were needed before attempting to clean a blood spill. From the counter in the examination room, I grabbed a pair of gloves. The car would need to be cleaned carefully before my children got in the car.

Upon my arrival at my mother's home, she brought me the towel to clean the car. When we looked at the blood, we were shocked. The back seat and the passenger side of the car had blood everywhere. There was blood on the dashboard and the windshield on the passenger side of the car. However, there was no blood near me, not one speck. There wasn't a trace of blood even on the back of my seat. Not a drop of blood was on my clothes. It was as if there was an invisible barrier that marked a point that the blood wasn't allowed to go beyond. My eyes began to cry unexpected tears.

"Something kept this blood from getting on me. There is something wrong with this blood."

My mother began to praise God for sparing me again.

"Thank you God for sparing my child again."

With her arms stretched towards heaven, she waved them in the night air. She also warned me that I needed to start thanking God for the things that He kept doing for me.

"You better learn how to thank God. He didn't have to spare you."

Continuing to cry, I carefully cleaned the blood and glass from the car. Immediately after Dee's stitches healed, we went back to our regular habits.

Buck remained out of town in hiding, and we seldom saw each other. One day, Dee and I decided to go to the city where he was hiding. This wasn't just for a visit. This was a good place for a shoplifting trip. We picked up Buck before we got started. Everything started out going well but as usual, we got greedy. Dee was an excellent thief but she had started slipping. When we got to the last store, Buck said that he was tired and didn't want to go in. This is the only time that can remember not wanting to take something. This should have been enough to change our minds. We proceeded into the store without him. Dee picked up something, and missed the buzzers. We had to run to the car. A Good Samaritan saw what had happened, and jumped in his car to follow us. Driving faster than I ever had, I was running lights and cutting in and out of traffic. The Good Samaritan was following right behind me. We traveled for several blocks, through congested traffic at this pace. He was determined to catch the car. Finally, he saw a policeman and flagged him down. When he stopped to explain to a police officer why he was chasing us, we got away. I had a spare tag in the trunk. Pulling onto a side street, we found an empty house where the tag could be changed. This was enough excitement for one day. We were ready to drop Buck off and then return to Columbus. My sentence was waiting for me if I got caught.

For years, I had been codependent, trying to make Buck stop using drugs. There was a constant fear that he would overdose. If he was away from home too long, I would go looking for him and bring him home. As he became accustomed to this practice, he learned to expect my arrival. This was a habit that was learned when I was six or seven years old. One of my dearly loved relatives was what can be referred to as a periodic alcoholic, because sometimes years passed without her drinking. She didn't drink often, but whenever she did she was unable to stop. The kids in the neighborhood teased Carlton and me about this. We would track her down at liquor houses (apartments in our neighborhood that sold alcohol). These weren't package stores, but rather people in the neighborhood who sold alcohol from their homes. When we found her we would try to make her come home. We would curse the people out and run tell my Aunt Pickle. They knew Pickle's attitude and reputation, so they wouldn't say anything to us. Pickle was sure to fight if they did. Whenever we did something bad we told Pickle. She would support us and sometimes, she gave us ideas. We didn't tell my mother because she would be embarrassed by our behavior. Neither would she tolerate this behavior from me.

This same codependent behavior was brought over into my relationship with Buck. One night he stayed out all night getting high. There was no doubt where he was, at his mother's house. All night long, I called trying to get him to come home but he wouldn't come. Finally, I decided to make him either paranoid enough or mad enough to come home. This is was sure to get a reaction from him.

"If you don't come home, I'm going to call your parole officer, and tell him how to find you."

This worked, and within ten minutes he was coming through the door. Buck wasn't prone to hit me. He has rather an even disposition and it takes a lot to make him mad. My mouth had provoked him to this point. When he came in the door, I was sitting on the sofa, anxiously waiting. I hadn't thought about what would happen once he got there. When he rushed at me with his hand positioned to strike, with reflex action my body balled up into a knot. There was no way that I was going to let him hit me with those big hands. His hands are twice the size of my hands. Out of fear, I kicked out of my fetal position prepared to run. This caught him off guard, and a 6'2", 225 lb. Buck fell backward onto the glass coffee table breaking it. My feet ran down the hall and out a side door. Behind me there was the sound of breaking glass. After getting up, he began breaking other things in the house.

With lightening speed, I ran across the street to Pat's house. Buck was right behind me. We both went straight to her bedroom. She was sitting on the side of the bed. Like a professional referee, she went to work.

"Calm down. What's wrong? Have a seat."

Since he hadn't hit me yet, I sat down on the bed, comfortable that he wouldn't hit me.

Again, Pat instructed, "Buck sit down."

He responded, "I can't."

She asked him why, and he turned around. He was wearing a navy blue and burgundy velour Christian Dior jogging suit. A chunk of meat was gapping through the cut in the back of his pants, and he was bleeding. He said he was going over to his mother's to get the wound bandaged. After he left in his car, I followed him in my car to his mother's house, a short distance away. His mother, sister, and brother-in-law were standing outside the house when I arrived. His mother and sister were really angry with me.

"You could have killed my son. I can't put a bandage on that. Take him to the hospital."

There was no response from me; she wasn't talking to me. She was talking more at me and instructing his sister to take him to the hospital. Anyway, Mama had trained me not to disrespect my elders.

In my mind the response was, "If he had hit me with that fist, he would have killed me. If you had sent him home none of this would have happened."

His sister was taking him to the hospital emergency room in Phenix City for treatment. When he got in the car with her and her husband, I got in too, sitting next to Buck. He didn't say anything. I didn't say anything. When we entered the emergency room, I walked to the desk with him, answering all the questions that they asked him. When they called him to the back room for treatment, I went quietly with him. While the nurse stitched him up, I watched quietly. Through the whole thing, Buck spoke as little as possible. He was no longer high. He was no longer angry with me. He remained quiet so no one else would know that; they were angry, but he had already forgiven me. When he left they instructed him to see a doctor in three to five days to have the stitches removed. In five days, I was the doctor that removed the stitches.

At this time, it was getting close to two years that I had been on parole. My parole officer told me that she was going to recommend that my sentence be commuted. This was something that I had never heard of, and never thought was possible. In my amazement, the part about this being a recommendation wasn't heard. With all of my gratitude and jubilation, I responded like my freedom had been granted that day. I would almost blow this recommendation before the process was complete. Since it was extremely difficult for me to see Buck with two parole officers checking on us, I thought it would be much easier if we moved. I mean physically moved the trailer. In a couple of days, the trailer was moved and painted a different color. We moved to different street in the same trailer park. This worked to keep the parole officers from finding us. This didn't stop my paranoia that they were going to catch us, especially after I had smoked a joint laced with cocaine. Buck would go to bed and leave me up worrying about this

It was going to take several months for my sentence to be commuted but this hadn't been shared with me. My parole officer came out looking for me but couldn't find the trailer, proving that she was justified in her recommendation. The next time I went in to report, she asked me what was my new address. She was told that I had moved in with my sister. She went out to my sister's house to check. This caught my brother-in-law off guard, because he didn't know that I had given their address and wasn't accustomed to these type situations. He told her that he didn't know Charlotte Russell. Later, an explanation would have to be provided to my parole officer. Additionally, before the sentence would be commuted, my stealing escapades escalated. Nevertheless, the sentence was commuted.

One day when I took Dee stealing, things went wrong almost immediately. The assistant manager was looking really strange. although nothing had been stolen.

Dee walked up to me and said, "Queen, I'm going to get you a mink coat."

Something didn't feel right.

I told her, "Don't do it. I think we need to get out of here."

Walking away, she said, "No Queen! I'm going to get you a mink coat."

The assistant manager looked directly in my face, something was wrong with the look that she was giving me. As I headed towards the door, the assistant manager paged the manager to the department. On his way to the department, he passed by me. I spoke to him and calmly made my way to the car. Looking through my rear view mirror, I observed that both the manager and assistant manager had walked out of the store looking for me. They were looking directly at me. My car was parked only two parking spaces from the front door of the store. They turned and went back in the store. They hadn't seen me. Again, God had spared me. The final paper hadn't been signed commuting my sentence. Looking for a better place to watch for Dee, I drove up a hill and parked where the store could be observed through the shrubbery. I called someone else to come to the store to check on her.

When he got to the store, the police were bringing Dee out. She was explaining that her disease made her do this. She later told me that she had told them that she had AIDS and was going to bite them. She said they didn't believe her. She said she was joking about having the virus. By the time Dee got to the jail, arrangements had been made for a bondsman to get her out. The bondsman was willing to allow us to bring the money back for the bond fee. When I picked Dee up, we did just enough stealing to get the money to pay the bondsman. Dee had actually been sick for awhile. This was just one of the few days that she felt well enough to go out.

In the mean time, my marriage was beginning to deteriorate rapidly. Things had reached a point where Buck and I no longer went on our missions together. Whenever I thought that he was coming home, I would leave. I was tired of living the way that we had been living for years. At night, sleep wouldn't come. Late one night, I observed a couple parking in a lot across from our trailer. This lot served as the parking lot for the trailer park's office, which had been closed for several hours. After parking the car, they walked down the street and out of my sight. My mind immediately went to parole officers. I went to each window in the trailer trying to recapture my view of couple. My searching included trying to catch a glimpse of these two people hiding behind one of the neighboring trailers. Buck went to bed, leaving me watching through the windows until the couple returned to my view, about 8:00 the next morning. As they drove off in the car, the realization came that they had their own secrets. All night long, it had been apparent that I was tripping. I just didn't realize the extent of the trip. Normally, the high didn't last this long. There was money, there were drugs, there were clothes, but they weren't free. The cost that they extracted was my peace.

Buck and I seldom talked to each other, passing only in the wind. Looking over my shoulders for police officers and parole officers was getting tiresome. My sentence had been commuted, but still the paranoia of police officers and parole officers remained. My frustration with Buck's drug usage was escalating. There was no sense of peace in our home. In the middle of the night, I would call Mama or Esther and tell them how troubled my mind was. There was no understanding of what was wrong with me. The money wasn't helping and the Marijuana wasn't making me laugh anymore. Reading the Bible wasn't working, because it seemed the words wouldn't come together to make a sentence. Nothing was alleviating my misery.

In the day of my trouble I sought the Lord: my sore ran in the night, and ceased not: my soul refused to be comforted. I remembered God, and was troubled: I complained, and my spirit was overwhelmed.

Thou holdeth mine eyes waking: I am so troubled that I cannot speak. Psalm 77:2-4

Things were getting worse. Dee had been sick for a while and the rumors were flying. It became apparent that she was really ill. She denied the rumor that she had AIDS, telling me once that she had been misdiagnosed. Once·while at our trailer, she walked off the side of the steps rather than walking down the steps. We couldn't understand why or how she had fallen. She had fallen flat on her face, but she wasn't hurt in the fall. Her memory became affected by what was going on with her. As time passed, I became more afraid that she was going to die. Deciding that I couldn't handle the possibility that she was going to die, my decision was to limit my telephone calls to Dee. This resulted in my hanging out with Betty regularly. The rumors about Dee began to escalate. My hopes were that somehow these rumors were wrong. Dee couldn't be dying from AIDS. There had to be a mistake. This couldn't be true. These were just cruel heartless rumors.

MARRIED TO THE BACKSLIDER

*I will heal their backsliding; I will love thee freely:
for mine anger is turned away from him.*

One morning, my mind began to dwell on Dee. I decided to call her. When she answered the telephone, she told me that she had been waiting for me to call her. She asked me to hold on while she hung up from her boyfriend, on the other line. This in itself was strange and troubled me. When she returned to the line, she informed me that her illness had caused her to forget my telephone number. I told her that I would get Buck to bring her a telephone that could be programmed to call me by dialing one number. It was then that she made the announcement that rang in my ears for days.

"I want you to know that I am HIV Positive, and I'm going to die within the next two weeks."

At this point, I was concerned about her soul, but I wasn't worthy to discuss Jesus or the blood that He shed for the remission of our sins. She had never been told that I was a backslider. This was part of my life that I was desperately trying to hide. There was never any doubt in my mind, that it was the Holy Spirit that talked to me, constantly warning me. Every time that I had gotten in trouble, the voice had warned me. Yet, I could only call Him "Something." This was because I wasn't ready to submit my will to Him. No matter how bad things got for me, no matter how many times I had been counted out, He had always pulled me out. I wasn't worthy to talk about Him. Now, I was faced with what was really the biggest challenge of my life. Dee had just said she was dying. I didn't want her to go hell, but I wasn't worthy to tell her how to be saved. There had to be a way to make sure she was saved without having to call His name.

For I am ready to be offered, and the time of my departure is at hand. I have fought a good fight, I have finished my course, I have kept the faith: henceforth is laid up for me a crown of righteousness, which the Lord, the righteous judge, shall give me at that day: and not to me only, but unto all them that love his appearing. II Timothy 4-7-8

Almost without breathing, I said, "If you feel like that, what have you done about it?"

Dee responded, "I have been praying."

I didn't even feel worthy to say pray, and so I responded, "What did you say?"

As if somehow understanding what I was trying not to say, she indulged me in a very foolish conversation. Wanting to be sure that she had indeed prayed a **PRAYER OF TRUE REPENTANCE**, after each statement, I asked an additional question.

"And how did you do that?"

After answering all the questions to my satisfaction, she told me, "I've fought a good fight. I'm tired. I've been dreaming about my grandmother. She was in a room, and there were a lot of steps that led to the room. I wanted to leave the room but my grandmother begged me to stay. She told me that if I left, I wouldn't be able to come back in. I didn't listen and I went out of the room. There were a lot of steps to get back to the door that led to the room but I wanted to get back in so bad. I kept knocking on the door. Someone opened the door and said, "He said knock and the door shall be opened." I'm ready to die. I just don't want to die alone. I know that I've done a lot of things wrong."

Sickness reminded me of my own struggle. I was afraid of people who were terminally ill. Afraid that their pain would cause me to relive my own. Later, the conversation with Dee was shared this information with Buck. Dee lingered on my mind all day, but I wasn't ready to deal with the possibility of her death.

The next morning while we were lying in bed, Buck turned to me.

He said, "CJ call Dee."

This scared me and it would take several minutes for him to convince me to pick up the telephone. Reluctantly, my fingers dialed the number. As the telephone continued to ring with no answer, my heart sank. Buck was trying to convince me to go to Dee's house to check on her. My preference was to keep trying to call her. Finally, he convinced me to go but only if he was going with me. As we were leaving the house, I decided to call again. This time Dee's mother answered the telephone. She told me that Dee was at the hospital and she was headed to the hospital. Afraid, I wanted to spend the day with Buck, but I wasn't about to tell him. Our days of even having polite conversations had passed. He went on his mission and I went on mine.

Usually, Betty and I went stealing together. We bought cocaine and marijuana after we peddled our goods. This had been our pattern for a couple of months. She lived in another nearby trailer park. Sharing whatever we had, we would split the money and drugs in half. She smoked her cocaine in cigarettes. My joints were sprinkled with cocaine. Usually, after we smoked one together, I would go home, that is unless Buck was there.

Once I returned home, Betty and I would talk on the telephone or should I say tripped over the phone. Betty was hiding from her parole officer, too. While I was no longer on parole, the parole officers were still looking for Buck. This didn't seem to bother him, but this stayed on my mind constantly.

> The way of peace they know not; and there is no judgment in their goings: they have made them crooked paths: whosoever goeth therein shall not know peace. Therefore is judgment far from us, neither doeth justice overtake us: we wait for light, but behold obscurity; for brightness, but we walk in darkness. We grope for the wall like the blind, and we grope as if we had no eyes: we stumble at noon day as in the night; we are in desolate places as dead men.
> Isaiah 59:9

The cocaine made us extremely paranoid. Most of the paranoia centered on fear of parole officers. Sometimes we worried about hidden cameras and police officers. But mostly it was parole officers. Whenever we were high, we imagined that the parole officers were at the door. The craziest part of this was that we were at least six blocks apart.

If I responded, "I hear somebody. I'm going to sit here quietly with the lights outs."

Over six blocks away, Betty would respond, "I hear them outside my door too. I'm going to do the same thing. I cut the lights out. If they don't hear anything maybe they'll go away."

We would hold the telephone, speaking only occasionally. However, this day since we were afraid that Dee was dying, we spent most of the day together, getting high, trying to numb the pain. We didn't want to be alone. Later that afternoon, Dee's mother called Betty's house to tell us that she had passed. She told us that Dee died lying in her arms. Dee was in pain, but after she took her last breathe a smile came across her face. The painkiller didn't work.

There would be several days before Dee would be buried. Betty and I were too upset to go stealing, but we had to find away to keep the painkiller going. This included doing things that I had never done. I had never gotten drugs on credit to get high, and had vowed never to try crack. The devil was having a field day with our minds. For me he was trying to destroy me with guilt. Each day was requiring more efforts to deal with the pain. The day before her funeral would be particularly difficult. We thought if we got high enough, we would be able to go view her body. Since we couldn't find any cocaine, we were willing to settle for crack. The guy who I went to for cocaine had known me for a number of years and was really reluctant to give me crack. Finally, after making me wait more than thirty minutes, he relented, giving me a small quantity of crack. We never managed to get high enough to go to the funeral home.

The next morning, I was really concerned about how I would be able to handle attending the funeral, without first seeing Dee's body. I hadn't been to a lot of funerals, and I wasn't looking forward to this one. My mother offered to go with me to the funeral home. When we arrived at Sconier's Funeral Home, a few blocks from my mother's house, I still wasn't ready to see her. While I remained outside of the door of the viewing room, my mother went in to view the body. She walked over to Dee's casket and after looking at Dee for a few seconds, she looked back at me.

She said, "Come on in to see her. She's beautiful."

There was a sound of reassurance in her voice that I desperately needed. Peeping from the door, I was able to get a glimpse of her and decided that I might be able to handle it. Slowly, I walked over to the casket, still afraid of something. I don't know what. However, there was something calming about looking at Dee's body lying there peacefully in the casket. To my total amazement, in death Dee looked better than she had in life. In spite of the illness, suffering, numerous years of substance abuse, and now death, she was indeed beautiful. God was going to make sure that I understood that this beauty wasn't the result of makeup.

There was another female body at the funeral home. In comparison to Dee there were some similarities and some vast differences. They were very close in age, but their lifestyles had been totally different. Whereas, Dee's life had been racked by substance abuse, sickness, and finally AIDS. This person had lived what is called the square life (meaning morally good or at least not obviously immoral). Yet, in their caskets, the two women were like night and day. Dee was a bright sunny day. So amazed by what we had seen, I asked the owner of the funeral home to take a picture of Dee for me. I wanted to remember how she looked forever. Later, there was a return trip to the funeral home to view her body with Betty. Since that day, the fear of death left me.

Betty and I drove to the funeral together, torn by our grief. On the outside we were dressed immaculately, looking like we had everything neatly tied together in a picture perfect package, inside we were more like used tissue paper. While the policeman led the funeral procession, we were drinking beer and smoking a joint. After the funeral, we decided to stop and get another bag of marijuana. Taking my last $20, I purchased the sack. In accordance with our usual routine, we split the bag. However, before we began smoking, Betty said that she needed to go to church the next day. Agreeing that this was a good idea, I told her that I would go with her. We had no real idea what church we were going to, but we were going. We decided not to smoke the marijuana until after we came from church. It just didn't seem right to go to church with a hang over. This is just an example of how much the devil had played with our minds. We had just left a funeral at a church and we were both high.

The next morning, I got up and put on my beige Harve' Bernard suit, an $800 suit Dee had gotten for me, and a Blue Fox coat. On the outside everything was all-together in my expensive clothes. On the inside everything was in disarray, and I didn't just feel cheap, I felt like trash. Buck was lying in bed looking at me. He knew that this was to early for me to be going stealing. The stores wouldn't open until 1:00. The look in his eyes was asking, "Where are you going?" The look that beamed from my eyes told him not to verbalize the question.

I left the house without saying one word to him. My anger about our lifestyles had reached the brink. Additionally, my desire was for him to feel the pain that I had felt for years, while he was out getting high, the pain of being his second love. Drugs were always his priority. I knew how to compete with a woman, but I didn't know how to compete with a spirit of addiction.

Oh, that you would listen to his voice today! The Lord says, don't harden your hearts as Israel did at Meribah, and as they did at Massah in the wilderness. For there your ancestors tried my patience; they courted my wrath though they had seen my many miracles. Psalm 95:7b-9 NLT

Betty and I rode around the city looking for a church to attend. After stopping at a couple of churches and ruling them out as possibilities, we ended up at my mother's church, my old church. There was a new pastor there, now. As we walked around the side of the church, unexpectedly, the familiar voice of "Something" spoke to me.

"It's over."

Mother Russell
And none of her words fell to the ground.

MAMA, WHY DO YOU STILL CARE

Yea, I have loved thee with an everlasting love:
therefore in love and kindness have I drawn thee.

The voice offered no explanations, only the simple declaration, "It's over."

There was no need for an explanation; I understood full well the implications of this statement. This revelation wasn't based on a sermon, a song, or a prayer. This was a direct revelation from God at a time when I least expected it. The only thing on my mind was my pain that I felt, the pain of losing Dee. There was also a lot of guilt. There were constant thoughts of things that should have been said to her. Was there a reason that Dee hadn't shared her illness with me? Had I done something to offend her or that caused her to feel that I would reject her? These were the things that were plaguing my mind. I wasn't planning to hear from heaven about my salvation. This wasn't what I was looking for. I just wanted the pain and the guilt to subside. However, God had other plans. My salvation was on His mind.

Can a maid forget her ornament, or a bride her attire? Yet my people have forgotten Me days without number. Jeremiah 2:32

"God I rejected you. I've tried to hide from your presence."

Like the father of the prodigal son, God had been waiting on me to come home. His arms were open wide, waiting to embrace me, waiting to welcome me back home. He was preparing a feast in my honor. He was giving me the best gift, the gift of eternal life.

Seek ye the Lord while he may be found, call ye upon him while he is near: Let the wicked forsake his way, and the unrighteous man his thoughts: and let him return unto the Lord, and he will have mercy upon him; and to our God, for he will abundantly pardon. For my thoughts, neither are your ways my ways, saith the Lord.
Isaiah 55:6-8

The God that is the God over time must have caused time to stand still. It took less than two minutes to walk to reach the front door of the church, but so much happened within this time. When He spoke those words, "It's over," I understood that I had run out of grace. I understood that I had exhausted the patience of God. I understood that before me had been placed a choice between life and death. There was a choice to be made between evil and good. Not only did I understand the choices, I understood the consequences. In the choices, there was actually only one choice. God was allowing me to choose my own fate. The answer was as clear as this scripture:

I call heaven and earth to record this day against you, that I have set before you life and death, blessing and cursing: therefore choose life, that both you and your seed may live. Deuteronomy 30:7

Additionally, God revealed to me how He had intervened on my behalf on numerous occasions. It wasn't that I was good at stealing or good at selling drugs that I had survived on the street. It wasn't because I was smart that I hadn't been sent back to jail or prison. It wasn't because I was careful that He had spared me from AIDS. It wasn't because I was strong that He had spared me from drug addition. I had taken every step to become hooked. It wasn't because I was lucky that my life had been spared numerous times. My life had been in danger more times than ever imagined. God revealed to me the times that He had intervened to spare my life. It was because of His grace that I had been spared. God knew the plans that He had for my life. I didn't.

For I know the thoughts that I think towards you, saith the Lord, thoughts of peace, and not of evil, to give you an expected end. Jeremiah 29:11

In my failure to acknowledge Him, somehow I thought that I had left Him behind. At this time, He was revealing to me that in every wretched thing I had done, He was there, sparing me from the consequences of my actions. He was letting me know that He would no longer interfere in my life if this was what I really wanted. The choice was mine to make. He was ready to withdraw His hand of protection from me, if I wasn't ready to willingly accept His intervention in my life. He had grown tired of my refusals to accept Him.

For innumerable evils have compassed me about: mine iniquities have taken hold upon me, so that I am not able to look up; they are more than the hairs on mine head: therefore my heart faileth me. Be pleased, O Lord, to deliver me: O Lord, make haste to help me. Psalm 40:12-13

Growing clearer to me was the damage who had been caused by my behavior. In my mind the only person who was being harmed by my behavior was me. My children always had their material needs met. They never saw me getting high. No one had been allowed to disrespect or abuse them. My mother had never seen me selling drugs or working the streets. It had never occurred to me to curse her out or beat her. All my behavior was away from her. Even in selling drugs, I had never introduced anybody to drugs. The people that I sold drugs to were already hooked. Even in my stealing, the stores were already over charging for the merchandise. They had insurance on the goods. The insurance companies were ripping people off, too. After all the rich were getting richer at the expense of the poor, and the poor were getting poorer. This wasn't fair. My actions were just helping to make things equal. This is what I was convinced of, until the scales fail from my eyes.

For the first time, I knew that I hadn't been a good mother. My children had suffered tremendous embarrassment and shame because of my activities. My children didn't want things they wanted me. They wanted to spend quality time with me. Additionally, there were other children being hurt. My selling drugs was helping to perpetuate the cycle of substance abuse. Drug addiction in those that I loved had caused me terrible pain, yet I had contributed to this same pain in others. Then there was my mother. This was the revelation that was almost too painful to bear. How could she still love me after all that I put her through?

A very shy and private person, she had been exposed to public shame because of what I had been doing. The things that were done had been horrible, but the rumors about what I was doing were often far worse. For years I had called on her to support me when I was scared or in trouble, but whenever the crisis passed I didn't want to be bothered with her. She had constantly tried to spare me the pain that was caused by my own actions, and I had resented this interference in my life. She later told me that at one point when she was witnessing to me, I asked her if she saw my name written in the Bible next to the scripture. This is something that I don't even remember, but I know that it's something that I said. I would never be able to bare my children treating me the way I had treated her. How could she still love me? I've never been able to figure this out. This remains a mystery to me.

My mother had never given up on me, even when there was no reason to believe that I would ever change. Inwardly bearing her pain, she had shown no sign of shame or embarrassment, because my conduct was constantly thrown in her face. She had stood faithfully by me during my darkest days. She had kept my children when I was running the streets, providing a safe haven for them. When I attempted to pay her, she had refused to take anything from my ill-gotten gain. This had deeply offended me. She had held on when there were no signs that I had any desire to ever change. How could I ever repay her for the humiliation and pain that I had put her through?

Time had to be standing still, because all of this was revealed unto me prior to my reaching the front door of the church. There was only a short distance from the parking lot to the front of the church, and inside the church the foyer was small. My decision had already been made before entering the doors of the church, if God would still have me, I was willing to surrender to Him. My will was causing me a lot of problems. There was no need for an inward debate with myself.

My brother and sisters, if anyone among you wonder away from the truth and is brought back again, you can be sure that the one who brings that person back will save that sinner from death and bring about the forgiveness of many sins. James 5:19 NLT

Dee had died at an early age, but this wasn't a wasted death. Her death had served as the final catalyst that would turn my life around. I was coming home for good. I was unable to make it on my own, and I was tired of trying. My life was out of control and I needed help. Mama wasn't surprised to see the prodigal daughter coming home. I was glad the doors were still open.

No Time to Waste

Redeeming the times because the days are evil.

The message that Sunday was "Interrupting Your Program for This Special Announcement." The message the next Sunday was "Can God Furnish a Table in the Wilderness?" Without a doubt I can tell you that He interrupted my program, and He knows how to furnish a table in a wilderness.

When we entered the church, we sat on the back row, not wanting to interrupt the service, not feeling quite comfortable being there. I don't think Betty had any idea what had happened to me on the way in the church, because she was dealing with her own internal war. I was tired of trying to run away from God. I had been a failure at this, too. Wherever I had gone, He was there.

Thou knowest my downsitting and my uprising, thou understandeth my thoughts afar off. Thou compassest my path and my lying down, and art acquainted with all my ways. For there is not a word in my tongue, but, lo, O Lord, thou knoweth it altogether. Thou hast beset me behind and before, and laid thine hand upon me. Such knowledge is too wonderful for me; it is high, I cannot attain unto it. Whether shall I flee from thy presence? If I ascend up into heaven, thou art there: if I make my bed in hell, behold, thou art there. If I take the wings of the morning, and dwell in the uttermost parts of the sea; Even there shall thy hand shall lead me, and thy right hand shall hold me. Psalm 139:2-10

My life would never be the same again. When I returned home, there were a couple things I needed to correct. The first thing I wanted to do was to assure that there were no drugs left in the house. After searching the house thoroughly, all the drugs were flushed down the toilet. Then all of my cigarette paper were located and disposed of, tearing them to pieces, making sure they would be no good to any one who happened to find them. There were several bottles of wine in the dining room cabinet. Each one of these was opened and the wine poured into the sink. After this was finished, I turned to my biggest challenge, trying to rectify the problems in my marriage.

This was well after time for the stores to open. Sunday was a short workday and you had to make your moves early, since the stores were open for only five hours. Normally, Buck would have been gone. His addiction wouldn't allow him to go for more than a few hours without his body going through withdrawals. The withdrawals weren't easy and they weren't pretty. Today, he was still in the bedroom waiting for me to return. The look that I gave him was totally different from the one that he had been given a few hours earlier. Tearfully, I apologized for trying to deliberately hurt him. He had done many things that had caused me pain, but they weren't done deliberately. Everything I had done for several months had been designed to hurt him and I had almost destroyed myself in the process. The next time I went to church he went with me.

> Howbeit when he, the Spirit of truth is come, he will guide you into all truth: for he shall not speak of himself; but whatsoever he shall hear, that shall he speak: and he shall show you things to come. John 16:13

God was working fast and He was restoring everything that I had allowed the devil to steal from me. We were broke but that didn't matter. We had something that we had never had before, peace. There were still challenges within our relationship that needed to be worked out. Whereas, I had zeal before without knowledge now the zeal was coming with knowledge. God had given me a spirit of thanksgiving, and beyond that He gave me a natural high. This one is better than the one that I was searching for with marijuana. Now I had the ability to laugh through almost anything, without the use of marijuana, and there would be no hangover.

> But then God our Savior showed us his kindness and love. He saved us not because of the good things we did, but because of his mercy. He washed away all of our sins and gave us a new life through the Holy Spirit. He generously poured out the Spirit upon us because of what Jesus Christ our Savior did. He declared us not guilty because of his great kindness. Titus 3:4-7a NLT

Buck was working, legally working, and he loved his job. He was actively involved in the church. About six months after having confessed that he had accepted Jesus Christ as his Lord and Savior, he was appointed a deacon. The missions looking for something steal had ceased, and his withdrawal from the heroin had gone smoothly and without any complications. Buck was no longer hiding. Nobody was looking for him. Whenever we saw detectives that knew Buck well, he would have conversations with them. Either, God had blocked the remembrance of the warrant for his arrest from their minds, or Buck's appearance was remarkably different, now that his system was clean from all the drugs.

Buck began to push me towards doing something constructive with my life. In doing this, he had no concept that he was opening up an old wound. These conversations were familiar to me. I remember the old conversations with my grandfather like they were yesterday, and my response was like this was yesterday. He really wasn't concerned about whether I went to school or went to work. His desire was that I do something positive with my life. This was viewed as his trying to shirk his responsibility for taking care of his family. I wasn't ready to secure employment or education. Physically and emotionally, I still needed a lot of work and healing.

It had been over a year that Buck had been free from active drug addiction. However, his appearance or behavior on drugs had never been forgotten. He began reading the Bible less, not that he ever been an avid Bible reader. Sometimes, he wouldn't come directly home from work. He began spending more time at his mother's house, and with some of his family members who were obviously not living for Jesus. His mother's house was part of his addiction playground. My suspicion was aroused, and suspected that he was dabbling with drugs again. However, when I checked his body for fresh needle marks, none could be found anywhere.

One night after I left church, I decided to go by Buck's job; this was well after time for him to be off. His car was there, but Buck had been gone for hours. Knowing that my suspicions were right about, I decided to teach another person to drive, Earline. Removing the key from my key ring, I placed it into the ignition and cranked the car. It was explained to Earline that there was no need to be afraid; Crystal had been taught how to drive using this same method. She was given the same instructions that had been provided Crystal years earlier.

"This is the brake and this is the gas. When you see my brake light come on put your foot on the brake. This is the signal. When I put my signal on you put yours on. Trust me and stay close to me. Don't be afraid. This is the way that I taught Crystal to drive a car."

We took almost the exact route that had been taken with Crystal, years earlier. From the rearview mirror, I observed her driving, and she was doing fine. She stayed close to me. Driving very carefully, we made it to the house. Earline told me she cried all the way home. I had prayed all the way home.

That night, Buck didn't come home, and I began packing his clothes. If there was anything that I was convinced of it was that there was no room in my life for this mess. I didn't want the spirits attached with the streets living in the house with me. The first hand knowledge that had been received about letting those demons that had been evicted move back in was still in the forefront of my mind. When Buck returned home, he was served his eviction notice. This was nothing new to him. There was no need for explanations.

A few days after he left, I became concerned about him. While convinced that he was abusing illegal drugs, there was something that just didn't add up. He continued going to work, and coming to church. Buck's heroin habit averaged between $300 and $500 a day. There was no way that a job could be supplying him with adequate money for this type of habit. Furthermore, the teaching that I was hearing convicted me about my actions. My decision was made to let him come back home. This started a pattern of me putting him out, being convicted for my actions, and telling him to come home. Finally, it was apparent what was going on with him. He had changed drugs. He was now using crack.

Buck had been protected by God's grace. However, he had chosen to walk from under the covering. The consequences of these actions were closing in on him. His nephew, Hatch had been in jail for about six months on a traffic violation. The time had passed for him to be released, but he remained in jail, unable to be released. Unbeknown to us, when Hatch was arrested, rather than giving his on name, he had given Buck's name. He was confined indefinitely under Buck's charges. With mixed emotions, the can of worms that had been packed away from view was opened.

The sheriff explained to me that he knew both Buck and Hatch well. He spoke to me over the telephone.

"I know who he is, but if he was stupid enough to use Buck's name, I'm not going to help him. Let him sit here."

Next, a call was placed to Hatch's probation officer to appeal to him for help. He agreed at my request to go to the jail to compare their fingerprints. There was one problem when he went make the comparison. Since Hatch had used Buck's name, all of the fingerprints under both names that were coming up belonging to Hatch. The probation officer didn't know how to correct the confusion.

With no other alternative, a telephone call that I really dreaded was made. Calling the District Attorney's office was really difficult, and I almost decided to leave Hatch in jail. When the first call was made, I don't think they believed my explanation of how the mix-up occurred. It took over a week to get someone to take the time to review all the charges that had ever been brought against each of them. Over the telephone, every attempt was made to help them distinguish who was the rightful owner of each charge.

About a week later, Buck's mother called to tell us that Buck's name was in the newspaper. Hatch had been released and the whole story was printed in the newspaper. For the first time in almost two years, that night I couldn't sleep. My thoughts were on parole and police officers coming to my house. It was as if the fear had never left me.

> *For as many as are led by the spirit of God, they are the sons of God. For ye have not received the spirit of bondage again to fear; but ye have received the Spirit of adoption, whereby we cry, Abba, Father. The Spirit itself beareth witness with our spirit, that we are the children of God.* Romans 8:14-16

When we paid the $10,000 to get Buck out jail on the possession charges, we had never planned on him going to court. The next day it was decided, Buck was going to turn himself in to face the charges. We met with our pastor to explain the circumstances. The pastor and most of the church agreed to support Buck through this process. Whenever Buck went to court on these charges, several members would take time off from work to provide support for him in the courtroom. Our pastor was there each time a hearing was held. He had a special fondness for Buck. Although, Buck was represented by a lawyer with a reputation for being one of the best in the city to defend these type cases, it was the church that represented Buck in the final analysis.

The DA (district attorney) wasn't inclined to give Buck a break on the sentence for these charges. The lawyer called my pastor and me outside the courtroom and told us what the DA was going to recommend to the judge. This sentence was unacceptable to both of us. The attorney didn't seem to care.

The attorney said, "Well you can attempt to make a statement to the judge, but normally the judge sides with the recommendation of the DA. I don't think it will help."

We wanted the opportunity to speak. The judge agreed to hear us, and each member of the church came forward to make a statement. As the presence of the Spirit of God filled the courtroom, a peace came over the courtroom. Everyone stopped moving, that is with the exception of the DA who was highly disturbed that this was being allowed. As each person began to speak in turn, the judge leaned forward attentively, and everyone else in the courtroom was silent. This seemed to anger the DA. It seemed that he was trying to cause a distraction by constantly pacing back in forth. If this was his aim, this didn't work. I seemed to be the only one watching him. After each of us had spoken, the judge rejected the DA's recommendation, cutting the recommended sentence in half. She sentenced Buck to three years. This was a miracle considering his record, and was the lightest sentence that he had ever received. The next day the headline in the local section of the newspaper read, "Local Judge Rejects DA's Recommendation."

Because thy lovingkindness is better than life, my lips shall praise thee. Psalm 63:3

My self-esteem had really been shattered by all the negative words that had been spoken over my life. For years, I had been wearing long sleeves and turtlenecks or dickeys. This had nothing to do with the weather. When the weather was hot, I continued wearing excessive clothes. While I liked nice furniture and my house clean, it was a real struggle for me to keep it clean. One day when I was attempting to clean the house, God began to clean me. He began cleaning me from the root of my hurt. In a way that only He can, He began to relate the struggle with the house with the struggle that I was having within myself.

And he answered and spake unto those that stood before him, saying. Take away the filthy garments from him. And unto him he said, Behold, I have caused thine iniquity to pass from thee, and I will clothe thee with a change of raiment. Zechariah 3:4

The shame that was felt when people stared at me caused me to feel like a freak. Always conscience that people were staring at me, the pain had been internalized. Additionally, I lived in fear that someone would find out about my checkered past, and reject me. The secrets that I was trying to hide made me feel dirty, used, abused, rejected, and neglected. It was too much to risk being hurt again. It was easier to remain trapped inside my comfort zone, hiding behind my clothes, hoping that no one would ever discover my dirty secrets. If it was left up to me, I was going to take my secrets, my pain, and my silent tears to my grave. There was too much to risk. There was safety inside my comfort zone.

God began to explain to me how good He had been to me in the midst of my worst trials. The glory of God had been revealed in His delivering me each time that I had been counted out. As for the turtlenecks and long sleeves, this was my shield and defense against the world. They said don't ask me what happened to me; the subject is off limits.

For years, whenever someone had asked me about the burns my choice was to ignore the question or change the subject. Whenever the burns were discussed, I was selective in what was told.

God said, "Tell the whole story; this is a way for you to glorify Me. In the midst of the fire, I was with you. In the midst of your recovery, I was with you. Whenever you tell it, tell the whole story."

By hiding behind my clothes, I was missing the opportunity to witness for Him. The dickeys were coming off. No longer would I wear long sleeves, as a necessity, each day. It took most of the day for me to clean the house. In the aftermath, walls had been washed, floors mopped, brass polished and crystal cleaned, all with my tears. My physical house and my spiritual house were cleaner than they had ever been. When the opportunity presented itself, I would be able to relate the whole story. This was only the beginning. Now that God was taking away the shame, I was moving towards fulfilling His purpose in my life. There was more that He was expecting from me. This was a small morsel for my journey, but for now this was enough. God was feeding me slowly.

> *And I thank Christ Jesus our Lord, who hath enabled me, for that he counted me faithful, putting me into the ministry; Who was before a blasphemer, and persecutor, and injurious: but I obtained mercy...*
> I Timothy 1:12-13

I knew God wanted me to do something but I didn't know what. My mother and I been faithfully ministering at the county jail for more than a year. She was now my best friend, and companion in the ministry. I was willing to share my experience in the street, during these Sunday visits, if this would help someone else. However, God wanted more from me. But what?

> *But he that knew not, and did commit things worthy of stripes, shall be beaten with few stripes. For* unto *whomsoever much is given, of him shall be much required: and of whom men have committed much, of him they will ask the more.* Luke 12:48

My daughter had wanted to be a lawyer since she was two years old. Now, that she was in the twelfth grade, it seemed that she thought the dream was out of her reach. Desperately, I wanted her to fulfill her goals. My life had been a failure, but I wanted more for her. All of my expectations for a better future were wrapped up in Earline. Somehow, I think she was watching my example rather than listening to what was said. I had given up doing anything professionally with my life. My contributions would center on my ministry. However, the more I began to push her, God began to impress upon my heart that I could do more. I had no idea what this could be.

There were still physical limitations in my body, and I lacked the education or experience that would qualify me for a decent job. In order to justify financially relinquishing my disability check, I needed to make more than minimum wage. Additionally, I wouldn't be able to work outdoors or anywhere that there would be extreme temperatures. The amount of time that would be required to sit or stand would have to be flexible. My reach and my ability to lift were still extremely limited. The range of motion in my neck was still constricted. Vocational Rehabilitation had worked with me several times but had been unsuccessful in resolving any of the barriers to my employment.

By this time, the inmates at the Muscogee County jail knew me better than most people. Mama and I had been going to the jail for several years, ministering to the female inmates. I decided to ask them what I could do to make a difference in the world, since I had no idea. There was almost unanimous agreement that based on my history, I would make a good AIDS or drug counselor. These choices seemed like good possibilities, and careers that might interest me. Therefore, there was a willingness to pursue these choices.

Having been out of the workforce for more than ten years, and drawing public assistance, I thought that somewhere there would be funds to help me get back into the workforce. My criminal history also concerned me greatly. This might be a major hindrance to anyone considering hiring me. Starting with Vocational Rehabilitation, I began looking for answers. My old counselor was still working there, so I went to see her for advice. Rather than offering help, she told me that this was a bad time for me to go into counseling, because the state was laying-off employees. She stated that there was no indication when this would end. From here, I went to the probation office. My old probation officer wasn't in, and the receptionist recommended that I speak to someone else. This was a mistake. The petite blonde sat behind her desk while I explained my situation to her. Afterwards, she looked down the endless tunnel that masqueraded as her nose, totally disgusted by my presence and situation, she gave me her answer.

She told me coldly, "With your record, you'll never be able to work for the state."

"Thank you."

Now our Lord Jesus Christ himself, and God, even our Father, which hath loved us, and hath given us everlasting consolation and good hope through grace, Comfort your hearts, and establish you in every good word and work. II Thessalonians 3:13

I walked away feeling somewhat dejected, but determined that she would be proven wrong. From there my journey took me to the Health Department to see June Wright. This was the first encouragement that was received in my quest to get my career on track. She told me what I so desperately needed to hear.

"You have the potential to do anything. Once, you go back to school never stop learning. Some places your past may hinder you, but there are other places that this will help you. Let me know what I can do to help you."

She had already helped me.

There was one other state agency that would need to be visited, the Department of Pardons and Parole. My parole officer was no longer employed with the agency. Therefore, I met with one of the men there who had a reputation for encouraging sincere changes in offenders. He held true to his reputation, and told me to find out what it would take for me to get a pardon. Afterwards, I spoke with one of Buck's former parole officers. After explaining to him what had happened in my life and the things I wanted to do, he told me that he would do what he could to help me, if I followed through on my plan. This was more than what was expected. Periodically, I would report to the office to let him know my progress.

It was time to find a school that would provide the educational foundation that would enable me to become a counselor. The first school that I stopped at was a two-year college. Their arrangements wouldn't suit my needs. They wanted me to borrow an excessive amount of money for my education. I was sure that there were funds somewhere to help me finance my education. I just didn't know where.

My fear of taking the SAT was still with me, and I was sure that at Columbus College, the examination would have to be taken. With nothing to loose, my decision was made to call the college. Due to the number of years that I had been out of school, I was exempt from the requirement of taking the SAT to be eligible for admission. The entrance examination would be all that I needed to pass in order to gain admission. This was something that I was confident that could be passed. They also had an Associates Degree Program in Mental Health program that was interesting to me. I wanted to become a counselor by the shortest route possible. There was no understanding on my part of what it would take for me to become a counselor. What I didn't know was that this program was being discontinued.

The college enrolled me in the Bachelors of Health Science Program without conferring with me. In the beginning the thought of having to attend college for four years was upsetting to me. There was no desire to attend college for four years. This seemed like an awfully long time in my calculations. Now that my mind was made up to go back to work, my desire was to do this quickly. So much of my life had been wasted frivolously, I didn't want to waste anymore time. I was ready to discontinue the public assistance that had been my crutch for a number of years. However, the change in programs was one of those things working out for my good. God was at work on my behalf. My limited knowledge just didn't understand this. My prayer had already become, "God help me to accept your will, even when I don't understand."

BETTER THAN BEST

And whatsoever ye do, do it heartily, as unto the Lord, and not unto men.

The program that I was trying to enroll in wouldn't have enable Jackie Titus to be my academic advisor. Nor would the program have allowed for the healing that I would get through participating in her classes. She would become the thrust to get me through the beginning of my educational and personal growth. Jackie Titus stood at a bridge called 'Brokenness' that had been bombarded with suffering and pain, beckoning for me to come across unto the shores of "Wholeness." Almost immediately, I told her part of my checkered past, leaving out the details that were still to embarrassing to be shared. She never flinched or showed any signs of shock. She consistently encouraged me to overcome my fears and doubts.

Ms. Titus had a rather unique teaching style that was just what I needed. In each of her classes, she added outside reading. From each chapter in the books that she assigned, she wanted you to learn something new about yourself. I thought that I knew myself fairly well. Ms. Titus would push me to learn more. This was something that wasn't comfortable and was fought against. However, if I was going to get A's from her classes, I would have to learn some new things about myself, painful things. This was made clear the first quarter.

Knowing all of the things that were stacked against me, I had decided that I would have to be better than the best. My goal was to graduate from college with all A's. Now, in my thirties, I felt that I had wasted most of my life. To make up for the years that I had wasted, I wanted to complete my degree quickly and by the shortest route possible. To complete this, I planned to take at least eighteen hours per quarter, and to go to school year round. Everyone in my family was asked to be patient until I finished my education. There would be time for us to spend quality time after I completed my education. It would take a lot of commitment on my part to reach my goals. They would need to be understanding and supportive. Now, that I had made up my mind I was going full force after my education.

During this time, I was praying and believing God for the outcome, but I was also doing everything that I could to ensure that I achieved my goals. This included studying every day of the week and as many hours of the day as it took to complete my assignments accurately. My confidence in my academic ability was still shaky. I had spent so much time doing just enough to get by that I had convinced myself that I couldn't do any better. I was also convinced that all the marijuana I had smoked had damaged my memory. It was going to take a major boost to my self-esteem to convince me that I had the academic ability to complete the program. God was immediately going to give me the victory to provide the boost that I needed to my confidence.

And whatsoever ye do, do it heartily, as to the Lord, and not unto men; Knowing that of the Lord ye shall receive the reward of the inheritance: for ye serve the Lord Christ. Colossians 3:23-24

The first quarter, I took English 101 and algebra and trigonometry from a graphic point of view. I was fairly confident of my ability to pass the English class. However, the math class caused me great concern. In addition to the formulas it would be necessary to master a scientific calculator. Each day, I sat a goal to complete at least one of the math problems. By noon, I was home each day from school. Immediately, I would begin working on the math problems. Earline was taking the same math, and was able to provide a lot of support. Sometimes, it would be well after midnight when I finished the first problem correctly. My diligence was rewarded. After taking almost four hours to complete the final examination, I earned my first "A." In the English class I made a "B." This was one of very few "B's" that I would earn. I had learned a valuable lesson. God gives us His best, but He expects our best.

God is our refuge and strength, a very present help in trouble. Therefore will not we fear, though the earth be removed, and though the mountains be carried into the midst of the sea; though the waters thereof roar and be troubled, though the mountains shake with the swelling thereof. Psalm 46:1-3

Physically, God blessed me too. The campus was very hilly, and attending classes on the campus would require me to do more walking than I had done since I had learned to walk again. The parking lots were a great distance from the classrooms. Before I started the college, I was unable to walk more than a block on a regular basis without becoming exhausted. My strength increased and I was able to make the daily tracks across campus without major complications. I only missed one day of school during my time at Columbus College. This was the day that I took my daughter to the University of Georgia for orientation.

Part of my academic program, included completing an internship at the Health Department in the Communicable Disease Clinic. After Dee's death, I had my first HIV test. I had been confident that I didn't have the virus because of the way God had protected me from exposure to the blood in my ignorance. Once I took the test I began to panic. Explaining to the counselor that I had just lost my friend to the virus alerted her to my concerns. During the days that I was waiting for my results, I worried her so much that we became friends. This led to my becoming actively involved in AIDS awareness and education. Over the years I insisted that Buck have several tests. They were all negative. The results weren't negative because of any precautions that we had taken. This was just another measure of the grace that God bestowed upon us.

As a result of my involvement with AIDS, I discovered that several people close to me had contracted the virus that causes AIDS. I was still actively involved with the jail ministry. When I arrived at the jail one Sunday, one of my close friends was in lock down. The third floor of the jail was designated for women prisoners. The floor was divided into three dormitory type cellblocks. Within each cell was two floors, eight rooms on the bottom floor, and eight rooms on the top floor. Originally, each room was designed to hold a single person. Due to the overcrowded conditions at the jail it was necessary for two people to share a room. Additionally, inmates who were unable to obtain a room had mattresses spread around the catwalk on the upper level of the cell. A metal door marked the entrance to each room. Each door contained a small shatterproof pane, and a metal flap at the bottom of the door. These flaps were normally locked, and the doors remained unlocked, unless there was a problem. Normally, disciplinary problems would cause an inmate to be isolated by locking them in the room alone. This time isolation was used for a different reason, a different purpose. It was used because of fear. When I asked why she was locked down, the answer came back.

"She just found out that she has AIDS. When the test came back positive, they sent her straight to isolation."

This time isolation was used because of the fear of AIDS. This disturbed me greatly, because I knew that this was a time when she really needed someone. I hadn't been there for Dee but I was going to be there for others who were suffering from a new kind of prejudice. Over the years, I have waited with several people through the last moments of their life. Hoping that my presence would provide a measure of consolation when their life on this side came to an end.

My soul shall make her boast in the Lord: the humble shall hear thereof, and be glad. O magnify the Lord with me, and let us exalt his name together. I sought the Lord, and he heard me, and delivered me from all my fears. Psalm 34:2-4

During my last year at Columbus College, I earned an academic scholarship from Kennon and Parker Realtors. I was selected to be a member of Phi Kappa Phi Honor Society. Also, I received the Bachelor of Science Honors Award. After three years at Columbus College, I graduated magna cum laude with a 3.64 grade point average on a 4.0 scale. Evelyn Russell's daughter had finally done something positive. Along with my husband, my mother, and my children, Ms. Titus was there to support me every step of the way. The people that I thought would support me when I began doing something positive with my life weren't there, but God sent others in their place.

During the time that I had been attending college, I continued to report my progress to the parole office. The best graduation present that I would receive was a recommendation to the Governor of Georgia that I be granted a full and complete pardon. Christmas 1994, I received the biggest Christmas present that I had ever received, a full and complete pardon from the governor of Georgia.

Two years later, I would return to college to earn my masters in Community Psychology in Counseling from Troy State University. In a year and a half, I completed this degree. Shortly after receiving this degree, I began working on a degree in Theology. Currently, I'm completing my M.Div. in Christian counseling at Beacon College and Graduate School. After Beacon completes the accreditation process for the doctoral program, I will enter the D.Min. Program. I have taken June's advice and decided to never stop learning.

In everything give thanks; for this is the will of God in Christ Jesus concerning you. I Thessalonians 5:18

While I was in college, I began working with a non-profit HIV education and prevention program. My salary was paid by a state grant. My first permanent job was in an office building next door to the blonde that looked down the endless tunnel that masqueraded as her nose, totally disgusted by my presence and my situation. Indeed the tunnel was too long for her to see the light at the end of it. She had been wrong in her prediction. I was working for a state agency, one of three state agencies that I have been employed by. Additionally, I have worked for three programs that received state funding.

I never knew Mr. Russell well enough for him to become my grandfather. He died before the Black Sheep was sheared and bleached. He died before I achieved all of his dreams for me. Most of his dreams were fulfilled in triplicate. He never saw me walk across the stage to receive my degrees. He missed it when I bought my house. He never saw me buy my first new car. He died without ever accepting me for who I was. He never saw what God saw in me. He died before his dreams became my dreams. Today he would accept me as his grandchild. Success didn't change me; I still have the heart of a champion, the champion of underdogs and black sheep. Only today, I defend the cause without accepting the title.

Good, better, best. Never let it rest until you good is better, and your better is best. I heard a representative from the Girl Scouts say this a few years ago, and it stuck with me. This is now my personal philosophy.

After all the struggles and trials in my life, it seemed to me that there would be a chorus of family and friends at each milestone, shouting, "Thank God! She finally did something right." This wasn't to be; with the exception of a few people who invested in the promise, God was the source of my strength and my refuge. My tears asked, "God why?" And it seemed to me, in the distance, I heard a chorus of Black Sheep shouting; "We made it over."

Brethren, I count not myself to have obtained anything forgetting those things which are behind, and reaching forth unto those things which are before, I press towards the mark of the high calling of God in Christ Jesus.

Philippians 3:13-14

REACHING BEYOND THE BREAK

They that be whole need not a physician, but they which are sick. But go ye and learn what that meaneth, I will have mercy, and not sacrifice: for I am not come to call the righteous, but sinners to repentance.

When I was child, even before I entered the second grade, my mother gave me a record player and it came with small records. There was one song I really liked. It was by Tommy James and the Shondells, "LIFE CUTS LIKE A KNIFE, I'M SO DEEPLY WOUNDED." This may not be the name of the song, but it was in the lyrics. Even at this early age it described my life, a life already plagued by a great deal of jealousy, resentment, and pain. I have devoted my life to helping others to reach beyond the breaks in their lives. I'm risking exposing my own pain to help others heal theirs. As I sometime tell my clients, "I'm giving out pieces of myself. Take the portion that you need and spit the rest out."

He has not punished us for all our sins, nor does he deal with us, as we deserve. For his unfailing love towards those who fear him is as great as the heights of the heavens above the earth. He removed our rebellious acts as far as the east from the west.
Psalm 104:10-12 NLT

Your life might not read like mine. You might even say, "I would never let a man beat me."

"I would never sell drugs."

"I would never let anyone use me like that."

"I would never tell my business like that."

"I would never forgive…"

"I would never…"

You might be able to say; "I wasn't born in sin or shaped in iniquity."

Or you might be able to say; "My righteousness exceeds that of the religious and political leaders of today."

You might be able to say, "My righteousness is exceedingly far better than a menstruating rag."

You may be able to say, "There is someone who would die for me, because I'm good."

And maybe you can say, "No corrupt communications ever proceedeth out of my mouth."

You might even say, "I have never sinned or come short of the glory of God."

If the walls in your life could talk, they might say of you, "The essence of perfection, example of righteousness, spotless and without blemish, sinless, generous, enthusiastic, law abiding citizen, Good Samaritan, family provider, wonderful devoted parent, loyal and faithful spouse, and that you have the patience of Job."

I would even venture to say that they might say, "From a youth he has kept all the commandments."

You might even be able to say, as one man did on his dying bed, "I've always been a good man. I have been faithful to my church. I've been a good father."

You might be able to sincerely say all these things. You might be right. You might... But, I doubt it. More than likely, if you have made these statements or had these thoughts, you are sincerely deceived.

> *If we say that we have no sin, we deceive ourselves, and the truth is not in us. If we confess our sins, he is faithful and just to forgive us our sins, and to cleanse us from all unrighteousness. If we say that we have not sinned, we make him a liar, and his word is not in us.*
> I John 1:8-10

Rather than saying, I don't understand, when we meet homosexuals, prostitutes, pimps, drug dealers, backsliders, or anyone who appears to be content without a relationship with God, we should remember the story of Hosea and Gomer. There was something painfully broken within Gomer. This caused her to look for satisfaction and happiness in worldly pleasures. Hosea continuously looked beyond her faults to see her needs. He did this by God's direction. This is a picture of how God looks at us in our fallen state. He looks beyond our brokenness to see what we have the potential to become for His glory.

We should forever remember the story of a love that reached beyond the break. We should be reminded to hear what the person isn't saying, that we too might reach beyond the breaks to restore fallen humanity. We are to reach below the surface to find the source of the hurt. If we find the source of the break, the hurt can be plucked up from the root. Once plucked up from the root, the source of the hurt/break can be destroyed. Once, this happens the cord can be mended together again. The person can then move beyond the break, and thus become a productive life for Christ. This person who has been forgiven much, will love much, and have a greater testimony for Christ. With the commitment and determination of Hosea, we should help each other reach beyond the breaks in our lives.

However, before we can reach beyond the break to restore others, we must reach beyond the breaks in our own lives. This is often a painful process. I am particularly fond of the prophet Hosea because his ministry reminds me of my own. Hosea had to live the message that he preached. Did knowing that God had a plan and purpose for the pain and humiliation that he endured lesson his own pain? I think not. Today, I encourage others to reach beyond the breaks, as I have had to reach beyond the breaks in my own life. Let me tell you what a break is. It's anything that seeks to keep you trapped in a place of complacency, destroying the purpose and plan of God for your life. In my own life one break led to other breaks that almost destroyed me. If it hadn't been for the Lord on my side, surely I would have been consumed by the multitude of my transgressions.

You may ask, "Am I my brother's keeper?" Without a doubt the answer is, "Yes!" When we are strengthened, we have a mandate to reach out ands strengthen our brothers and sisters. Salvation is free but in order to maintain our salvation, we must give it away to others. We have to be real with God and with our selves. He already knows the source of our pain, but He can't heal a lie. We have to tell Him where it hurts and why it hurts. Then and only then can God heal the pain. Then we can use the experiences of our pain to help our brother and sisters overcome their pain. It might be a different type pain, but the wound needs healing. With the same comfort that God has given us, we can comfort others, if we are willing to take the risk of appearing weak. My motto is: if all I take away from my experiences is pain and tears, the pain has been wasted.

Once we have been healed we have a command: When thou art converted strengthen thy brother. Somehow we have missed this commandment. So many times rather than building up, we tear down. Rather than looking down to help others up, we look down to see if there is any body beneath us, and if they're not far enough down, we push them lower. Why? Because somehow it makes us feel better about ourselves when we look down on others. This assures us that we aren't on the bottom of the barrel. WHY? In the shelter of our insecurities, we hide under the shadow of the failures of others. If only we could be real with God, and risk being made free.

> How long, O Lord? How long will the wicked be allowed to gloat? Hear their arrogance! How these evil doers boast! They oppress your people, Lord, hurting those you love. Psalm 94:3-5 NLT

Recently, I went through a trial and I was plagued by thoughts of people actually rejoicing over what appeared to be my downfall, or thinking once again that I had been counted out. I had been knocked down, but not out. I was reminded of the pain and agony that Jesus suffered on the Cross. He endured a horrible, agonizing, and humiliating death. He was willing to do that because He loved me. Not the "Me" that exist today, but that other "Me," The one that only Jesus would think about dying for. Once again, He reached beyond the break to restore me.

My life has gone through numerous changes in the years since I have been saved. Every day hasn't been easy. There are times when I don't understand what God is doing in my life. I have learned to pray, "God help me to accept your will, even when I don't understand." There are still areas in my life where God is working out the glory.

The seeds of disobedience that I sowed had to be reaped; although, my daughter says 'the reaping' really wasn't that bad. The reaping was extremely painful, knowing that I caused my own pain. Herman picked up a lot of my habits. There were constant calls from the schools about things that he was doing. He did very little to apply himself academically. My efforts to refine his behavior were unsuccessful. My love for Marijuana was passed on to him. There were times that it appeared that he hated me. He refused to come home at any decent hour. His friends were the ones that break a mother's heart. It would have been easier if I could have said he was just like his father, but I refused to speak this curse over his life. In actuality, he's just like his mother.

My mother has a love for oriental rugs. One Saturday afternoon, she was nagging me about taking her to buy one of these rugs. Rather than doing this, I stopped to have my nails done. Not to be thwarted, she continued talking about the rug. This is just her way. Finally, I told her that if she weren't afraid, she would let Herman take her to pickup the rug. This was supposed to be a joke, because Herman had never driven a car in the road. He had only pulled a car into the driveway.

Herman asked me to give him the keys. I gave them to him, still thinking that we were joking. Mama went out the door with him and got in the car. In my mind, surely he wouldn't drive off in my car. To my utter dismay, Herman drove the car unto one of the busiest street in Columbus. Mama has been driving for years, but was afraid to drive on this street.

Mama said when she told Herman to stop at the red light, he responded, "I've never done that."

They made it safely to the store, but Mama was realizing the danger that they were in. She told Herman to tell me to come pick her up, because she wasn't riding back with him. Mama was so scared that she had forgotten that she could drive. Realizing he was scared, reluctantly, she got back in the car, with Herman behind the steering wheel.

When they returned to the nail salon, Herman asked, "Where do you want me to park?"

Relieved that they had made it back, Mama responded, "Anywhere."

It was this experience that caused me to look at Herman differently. The problem was that he was just like me. He had inherited most of my bad habits, and all of my good habits. Wrestling with his behavior was like wresting with myself. I realized that he was my child, and as such he needed a lot of love. He needed to be accepted for who he was. I stopped trying to change him, and started working on accepting him. This didn't mean that I liked the behavior. Nor did it mean that I stopped fussing. It simply meant that I was going to patiently wait for the change to come. Verbally, I began to say he was changing. My words began to speak blessings into his life.

A couple of months later, he got in trouble at school and I made a desperate decision to pull him out of school. Herman was in the ninth grade and showing no efforts to pass on to the tenth grade. The school district wanted to send him to the alternative school. I informed them that Herman wouldn't be returning to public school. A month later, I made preparations to send him off to the Job Corps in North Carolina.

Not wanting to go, Herman said, "Mama I want to go back to school."

As I looked in to the eyes of my baby, I almost changed my mind, but I was resolved to do what was best for him.

Resolutely I told him, "You are my child but you don't have to make my mistakes."

This was turning point for both of us. Rather than getting frustrated with his behavior, I began to deal with him the way I dealt with myself. Talking to him and punishing him wasn't going to work; he would have to learn from his own mistakes.

Herman arrived safely at the Job Corps, in spite of several adventures that he took during the bus trip. He wasn't prone to go directly anywhere, and each time that the bus would stop, he went exploring his surroundings. The week that he arrived at Job Corps, he went through diagnostic testing. He only missed one question out of all his tests. The next week, he passed the GED exam. Then I began making arrangements for him to come home to take the SAT. On his first weekend pass, I took him to a college in Atlanta where he made a 1000 on the SAT. This was remarkable, since, he had never given any effort to learning anything, and hadn't completed the ninth grade. At sixteen, he began attending college in Atlanta, but all he wanted to do was collect telephone numbers. Later, I transferred him back to Columbus. I was tired of worrying about where he was at night. Herman is now in Columbus attending Beacon College and Graduate School. At eighteen, God beautifully saved him.

When I think about the things that I have endured, the things that my mother endured, and so many other mothers are enduring, I am reminded of another mother. A mother that was raised in a place that can only be called a ghetto. A mother who became pregnant out of wedlock, while attending church. A mother that was subject to public embarrassment and scrutiny. A mother who almost lost her fiancé. A mother who bore her child into poverty. A mother who didn't have a Ginny Linn crib or pastel baby clothes. A mother who didn't have a private suite available for her child's birth. A mother who didn't have a private physician. A mother who couldn't pay large tithes. A mother who received a prophecy that she was going to suffer. A mother whose child was missing for three days. A mother who watched when her child was being talked about and rejected. A mother who watched her child being used for what he had to offer. A mother who watched her innocent child being jailed. A mother who watched while her child was beaten with whips. A mother who watched her son carrying the weapon that would be used as the instrument of his death. A mother who watched when a thorn of crowns was forced on her son's head. A mother who watched when her son was mocked and scorned. A mother who watched as her son was nailed to the cross. A mother who watched her son die, an innocent man. A mother who watched when her son died without her dreams for him being fulfilled. It's Mary the mother of Jesus that I think about.

Mary was part of a generation that was looking for a redeemer and a savior to come with a sword and shield, revenging them of their enemies. She had accepted the promises of God. She had born the Promised Seed, but now the promise was gone, without reeking vengeance on the enemies of Israel. Perhaps Mary didn't understand. Perhaps she thought all of her suffering had been in vain. Yet, she was one of the people choosing to wait in the upper room for the promise to come. She saw the promises of God revealed on the day of Pentecost. Now, she understood that her suffering hadn't been in vain. She understood more perfectly the plan of God.

Who has believed our report? And to whom is the arm of the Lord revealed? For he shall grow up before him as a tender plant, and as a root out of dry ground: he has no form nor comeliness; and when we shall see him, there is no beauty that we should desire him. He was despised and rejected of men; a man acquainted with sorrows, and acquainted with grief: and we hid as it were our faces from him; *he was despised, and we esteemed him not. Surely he has borne our grief, and carried our sorrows: yet we did not esteem him stricken, smitten of God and afflicted. But he was wounded for our transgressions, he was bruised for our iniquities: the chastisement of our peace was upon him; and with his stripes we are healed. All we like sheep have gone astray; we have turned everyone to his on way; and the Lord has laid upon him the iniquity of us all.* Isaiah 53:1-6

Whom The Son has
set free, is free
indeed.

EPILOGUE

In writing *To Hell and Back*, I had to relive the things that I had chosen to forget, particularly in the burning bedroom. At another point in my life, this memory would have been intolerable. Today, God has given me the strength to cope with the memory. I'm still not worthy of all the love God's shown to me. When I think about myself, I can only describe myself as GRACE. God's Amazing Grace. I live in place beyond Faith called Grace. This is a place where I accept His will over my will.

I'm still learning to forgive myself for the things that I did against God and my mother. My mother has become my closest companion. Although, she constantly reassures me that I have made her last days her best, I have never been able to forget the depth of the pain I caused. The healing is still in process. We are still partners in ministry.

In spite of the discouragement that I received, I have worked a number of jobs for the State of Georgia. I have worked with numerous community organizations, particularly as it relates to AIDS and substance abuse. Working has provided a new set of challenges. Therefore, I have strayed away from this subject. The lessons that I have learned in the workplace have been unique. Sometime in the near future, I'm sure God is going to use these experiences for His glory.

Physically, occasionally there are still challenges in my body, but His grace is sufficient for me. A few years ago, I was dancing in church and God performed cosmetic surgery on my chest. The miracle was complete, and on the way home I had to stop to purchase an article of clothing that I hadn't needed in years. I was glad that I never had the implants.

Herman is a soul winner and a prayer warrior. I struggled with Herman for a number of years, until I realized the problem was that he was like me. This insight removed some of the frustration, but not the pain. He has a beautiful sweet spirit.

My daughter has completed two B.A. degrees from the University of Georgia, one in Religion and another in Sociology. She's currently working on a third degree, a master's in Social Work with a minor in Law. She's planning to enter law school next year. She is also working for the State of Georgia. Herman says Earline is coming home to the Lord soon.

My beautiful granddaughter, La'Toya is the joy of my life. She lives in Athens, Georgia. She left me her dog, Hero.

My mother spends almost every day with me. We're working to recover all the years that the cankerworm had stolen from us.

God is working on me to be the person that I should be. I have stopped asking Him to fix Buck, and started praying for Him to fix me. God is still working out the glory.

Crystal now has five children, two boys and three girls. She gave each of the girls part of my name. I'm her hero.

Aunt Bobbie has in the last years struggled with major health problems. She gave up drinking and smoking cigarettes years ago. Her sense of humor hasn't changed, and occasionally, she still thinks she's my mother.

Sonya married the guy that she was slipping off to see, Phil. They have three children and two grandchildren.

Robert hasn't changed in attitude or behavior. His appearance, now virtually destroyed by years of alcohol abuse, has ended his days of womanizing. His body is frail and weak from alcohol abuse and his ability to perform even a menial work related task severely impaired.

Jim was recently released from prison. While there, he did extensive Bible study and confesses that he has accepted Jesus Christ as his Savior.

Chuck died three months ago. He never stopped loving or encouraging me. His love was unconditional, loving me not only at my best, but when I was at my worst.

My Uncle Carlton lived with my grandmother most of his life, never being able to marry or having children. In a lot of ways mentally, it was like he stopped growing at seventeen. He has Ma'Dear's sweetness of spirit. A year before Ma'Dear passed, Carlton began thinking about what would happen to him if Ma'Dear passed. Without anyone in the family being aware of his intentions, he made arrangements to move into semi-independent living program. He's now my third child.

Buck is still trapped in his own world and suffering the consequences for his behavior.

Ma'Dear passed last year, a month after she was diagnosed with Cancer. Mama was holding one hand, while I held the other. My uncle was holding her feet.

Although God impressed upon my heart a number of years ago to write this book, I put it off as long as I could. Now that I have been obedient, it is my prayer that it will fulfill the purpose that He intended. As high, the heavens Lord your name I proclaim. To You be the glory, the honor, and the praise, both now and forever. AMEN.

Reaching Beyond the Breaks
www.reachingbeyond.net

Helping hurting humanity to reach beyond the barriers in their life, one barrier at a time.

ORDER FORM

Know someone else in crisis, or in need of encouragement order additional copies of this book to sow seeds of healing grace.

Postal Orders:

Reaching Beyond the Breaks Ministries
P. O. Box 12364
Columbus, GA 31917-2364
(706) 573-5942
Email us at: admin@reachingbeyond.net

Please send the following book(s). I understand that I may return any books for a full refund-for any reason, no questions asked.

Qty.

_____ ***A Journey: To Hell and Back***,
   by Charlotte Russell Johnson $14.95 each

Sales tax:
   Please add 7% for books shipped to Georgia addresses.
Shipment:
   Book rate $2.50 for the first book and $1.00 for each additional book.
Payment:
   ☐ Check
   ☐ Money order

Also available at www.amazon.com